Pillsbury

COOKIE RECIPES TO TREASURE

Ottenheimer Publishers, Inc.

Publisher: Ronald J. Kos
Managing Editor: Diane B. Anderson
Associate Editor: Elaine Christiansen
Subscription Coordinator: Vicki Kuhlmann
Publications Assistant: Karen Goodsell
Food Editor and Food Styling Assistant: Lola Whalen
Food Stylist: Lynn C. Boldt
Contributing Editor: Heather Randall King
Home Economists: Pillsbury Consumer Center
Nutrition Coordinator: Patricia Godfrey, R.D.
Design, Production: Tad Ware & Company. Inc.
Photography: Studio 3

Cover Photo: Crisp Chocolate Snaps and Ginger Cookies p. 24.

Contents

BAKING TIPS FOR COOKIE BAKERS

Cookies and bars, favorite foods the world around are wonderfully easy and tempting for home baking! The few tips included here can help to make your homemade cookies the very best ever.

First and foremost, all INGREDIENTS should be fresh. Keep tabs on freshness by checking the expiration dates stamped on packages.

Our recipes usually call for BUTTER or MARGARINE. For easy measuring, cut off the amount needed from a refrigerated block or stick. When SOFTENED BUTTER or MARGARINE is called for, it should be soft enough to blend smoothly with other ingredients. Do not soften by melting and do not substitute oils or whipped butter or margarine products. If recipe calls for SHORTENING, use solid hydrogenated shortening from a can.

EGGS add moisture, richness and body. They should be large-size for our recipes and have clean, unbroken shells. Separate yolk from white when egg is cold. EGG WHITES offer better volume and texture if at room temperature before beating.

Pillsbury FLOUR does not require sifting before measuring unless recipe indicates. Measure flour by spooning it lightly into a dry measuring cup; level off with knife or spatula.

Our recipes use double action BAKING POWDER and BAKING SODA as leavening agents. To perform properly, baking powder and baking soda should be used before expiration date and stored in a cool, dry place.

GRANULATED SUGAR should be dry and lump-free. Measure sugar as directed above for flour. Store in an airtight container in a cool, dry place to prevent lumping.

BROWN SUGAR is measured by *firmly packing* lump-free sugar into a dry measuring cup. Keep it soft and lump-free by storing in an air-tight container.

POWDERED SUGAR is finely pulverized granulated sugar with a small amount of cornstarch added. It is generally used in frostings, glazes and coatings or sprinkled over baked products. Measure powdered sugar as directed above for flour. If powdered sugar is not lump-free, sift before measuring for accuracy and smooth consistency.

Melt CHOCOLATE in microwave oven or in heavy saucepan over low heat, stirring frequently. Do not allow steam or water to come in contact with chocolate or the mixture may "stiffen" or "set," making it difficult to mix with other ingredients. If melting chocolate does "stiffen," correct the texture by stirring in small amounts of solid hydrogenated shortening—about 1½ teaspoons for a half-cup of chips or 3 ounces of squares. Do not use oil or butter-flavored shortening for this process.

Purchase NUTS which have not exceeded the expiration date and are tightly sealed. Stale or rancid nuts give batters an "off" flavor. Store nuts in an airtight container in a cool, dry place. We recommend chopping them with a nut chopper or rotary-type grinder designed specifically to cut nuts sharply and keep them dry. A blender or food processor tends to bring too much oil out of the nut meats and can result in a paste-like texture.

MICROWAVE-EASY TIPS FOR COOKIE BAKERS

Remember that oven wattages and cooking patterns vary. The suggested times below are GUIDELINES and may not be exact, depending on your particular oven. We suggest you check foods at the first doneness time given and make adjustments as needed.

MELTING CHOCOLATE:

Place chips or squares in a microwave-safe container. Microwave on MEDIUM, stirring once during process.
- One 1-ounce square for 1½ to 2 minutes
- Two 1-ounce squares for 3 to 4 minutes
- One 6-ounce bag chips for 2½ to 3 minutes
- One 12-ounce bag chips for 5 to 6 minutes

MELTING CHOCOLATE WITH BUTTER OR MARGARINE:

Place in a microwave-safe container. Microwave on HIGH without stirring for 1½ to 2 minutes for 2 squares of chocolate. Stir and microwave slightly longer if necessary.

SOFTENING BUTTER OR MARGARINE:

Place one refrigerated stick in a microwave-safe container. Microwave on HIGH 5 seconds; let stand 15 seconds. Repeat timings until butter is just *softened, not melted.*

SOFTENING CREAM CHEESE:

Remove foil wrapper from a chilled 8-ounce package. Place in microwave-safe container and microwave on HIGH for 30 to 45 seconds.

PREPARING COOKIES FOR MICROWAVING:

Arrange 6 to 9 dough pieces in a circle on a greased microwave-safe baking sheet or suitable plate. Molded and drop cookies should be 2 inches apart; other types can be closer together.

Do not cover before microwaving.

Follow recipe timings and rotating instructions. Some cookies may cook faster than others, depending on oven pattern. Remove any with a dry surface—a sign of doneness. Cookies will not brown, but they should lose doughy appearance when cooked.

Remove from oven and allow to set briefly before removing from pan.

Easiest-Ever
DROP COOKIES

Easiest-Ever
DROP COOKIES

For filling that cookie jar FAST...

Easy to make—easier to eat, drop cookies immediately come to mind when we want homemade goodies in a hurry. Made from quickly-combined ingredients and dropped swiftly from a spoon, these popular treats offer enticingly endless flavor and texture choices. Soft or crisp, crunchy or chewy, drop cookies can be baked conventionally, in the microwave oven or not at all in some super-speedy recipes.

In answer to many consumer requests, we have developed several outstanding recipes using cake or brownie mix as the "magic" ingredient. So streamlined for busy bakers, these gems are every bit as delicious as "scratch" versions.

If you're partial to nutritious ingredients, look no further. We have recipes featuring whole wheat flour, oats, fresh and dried fruits, cereals, wheat germ, peanut butter, yogurt—even carrots and zucchini! These good-for-you ingredients become irresistible when creatively combined with favorite spices, chocolate, coconut, nuts, preserves and other inviting additions.

Most drop cookies freeze well when properly wrapped and defrosting takes only 20 minutes or less. Store cookies in a tightly-covered container unless recipe recommends otherwise.

A double chocolate oatmeal cookie with a special crunch from packaged cereal.

Chocolate Oat Chipsters

¾ cup firmly packed brown sugar
½ cup sugar
¾ cup margarine or butter, softened
2 oz. (2 squares) unsweetened chocolate, melted, cooled
1 teaspoon vanilla
2 eggs
1 cup Pillsbury's BEST® All Purpose or Unbleached Flour
½ teaspoon baking soda
½ teaspoon salt
2 cups rolled oats
1 cup crisp rice cereal
6-oz. pkg. (1 cup) semi-sweet chocolate chips
½ cup chopped nuts, if desired

Heat oven to 350ºF. Lightly grease cookie sheets. In large bowl, beat brown sugar, sugar and margarine until light and fluffy. Add chocolate, vanilla and egg; blend well. Lightly spoon flour into measuring cup; level off. Stir in flour, baking soda and salt; mix well. Stir in oats, cereal, chocolate chips and nuts. Drop by rounded teaspoonfuls 2 inches apart onto prepared cookie sheets. Bake at 350ºF. for 9 to 13 minutes or until set. Cool 1 minute; remove from cookie sheets. 4 dozen cookies.

HIGH ALTITUDE—Above 3500 Feet: Increase flour to 1 cup plus 2 tablespoons. Bake as directed above.

NUTRITION INFORMATION PER SERVING

SERVING SIZE: 1 COOKIE		PERCENT U.S. RDA PER SERVING	
CALORIES	110	PROTEIN	2%
PROTEIN	2g	VITAMIN A	2%
CARBOHYDRATE	13g	VITAMIN C	*
FAT	6g	THIAMINE	4%
CHOLESTEROL	10mg	RIBOFLAVIN	2%
SODIUM	80mg	NIACIN	*
POTASSIUM	60mg	CALCIUM	*
		IRON	2%

*Contains less than 2% of the U.S. RDA of this nutrient.

In answer to many consumer requests, we have developed a cookie from brownie mix. The results are so good we think you will want to keep a box on hand just for these quick mix treats.

Brownie Chip Cookies

21½-oz. pkg. Pillsbury Family Size Deluxe Fudge Brownie Mix
⅓ cup margarine or butter, melted
2 eggs
6-oz. pkg. (1 cup) semi-sweet or milk chocolate chips

Heat oven to 350ºF. Generously grease cookie sheets. In large bowl, combine brownie mix, margarine and eggs; beat 50 strokes by hand. Stir in chocolate chips. Drop by rounded teaspoonfuls 2 inches apart onto prepared cookie sheets. Bake at 350ºF. for 8 to 12 minutes or until set. Cool 1 minute; remove from cookie sheets. (Cookies will flatten when removed from oven.) 3 dozen cookies.

HIGH ALTITUDE—Above 3500 Feet: Add 2 tablespoons flour to dry brownie mix. Bake as directed above.

NUTRITION INFORMATION PER SERVING

SERVING SIZE: 1 COOKIE		PERCENT U.S. RDA PER SERVING	
CALORIES	110	PROTEIN	*
PROTEIN	1g	VITAMIN A	*
CARBOHYDRATE	16g	VITAMIN C	*
FAT	5g	THIAMINE	2%
CHOLESTEROL	15mg	RIBOFLAVIN	2%
SODIUM	85mg	NIACIN	*
POTASSIUM	40mg	CALCIUM	*
		IRON	2%

*Contains less than 2% of the U.S. RDA of this nutrient.

Shown on pages 4 and 5 —
On rack (L to R): Brownie Chip Cookies pg.7, Whole Wheat Zucchini Cookies pg.18, Chocolate Oat Chipsters pg.7

Duplicate those large, crisp, chocolate chip cookies from the cookie shops and their memorable flavor using this special recipe.

Chocolate Chip Cookie Giants

¾ cup sugar
½ cup firmly packed brown sugar
¼ cup chocolate flavor drink mix
1 cup margarine or butter, softened
1 teaspoon vanilla
2 eggs
1½ cups Pillsbury's BEST® All Purpose or Unbleached Flour
1 teaspoon baking soda
½ teaspoon salt
1½ cups quick-cooking rolled oats
12-oz. pkg. (2 cups) miniature semisweet chocolate chips

Heat oven to 375°F. Lightly grease cookie sheets. In large bowl, beat sugar, brown sugar, drink mix and margarine until light and fluffy. Add vanilla and eggs; blend well. Lightly spoon flour into measuring cup; level off. Stir in flour, baking soda and salt; mix well. Stir in oats and chocolate chips. Drop by rounded tablespoonfuls 3 inches apart onto prepared cookie sheets; flatten slightly. Bake at 375°F. for 9 to 12 minutes or until light golden brown. Cool 1 minute; remove from cookie sheets. 2½ dozen cookies.

HIGH ALTITUDE—Above 3500 Feet: Increase flour to 1½ cups plus 2 tablespoons. Bake as directed above.

NUTRITION INFORMATION PER SERVING

SERVING SIZE: 1 COOKIE		PERCENT U.S. RDA PER SERVING	
CALORIES	200	PROTEIN	2%
PROTEIN	2g	VITAMIN A	4%
CARBOHYDRATE	24g	VITAMIN C	*
FAT	11g	THIAMINE	4%
CHOLESTEROL	20mg	RIBOFLAVIN	2%
SODIUM	150mg	NIACIN	2%
POTASSIUM	90mg	CALCIUM	2%
		IRON	4%

*Contains less than 2% of the U.S. RDA of this nutrient.

No need to shape the dough for this thumbprint cookie. Just drop onto the cookie sheet for a melt-in-your-mouth poppy seed cookie with a filling of cherry preserves.

Cherry-Poppy Seed Twinks

1 cup powdered sugar
1 cup margarine or butter, softened
1 teaspoon vanilla
1 egg
2 cups Pillsbury's BEST® All Purpose or Unbleached Flour
2 tablespoons poppy seed
½ teaspoon salt
⅓ – ½ cup cherry preserves

Heat oven to 300°F. In large bowl, beat powdered sugar and margarine until light and fluffy. Add vanilla and egg; blend well. Lightly spoon flour into measuring cup; level off. Stir in flour, poppy seed and salt; mix well. Drop by rounded teaspoonfuls onto ungreased cookie sheets. With finger, make imprint in center of each cookie. Fill each imprint with about ½ teaspoon preserves. Bake at 300°F. for 20 to 25 minutes or until edges are light golden brown. Immediately remove from cookie sheets. 2½ dozen cookies.

HIGH ALTITUDE—Above 3500 Feet: No change.

NUTRITION INFORMATION PER SERVING

SERVING SIZE: 1 COOKIE		PERCENT U.S. RDA PER SERVING	
CALORIES	110	PROTEIN	*
PROTEIN	1g	VITAMIN A	4%
CARBOHYDRATE	12g	VITAMIN C	*
FAT	7g	THIAMINE	4%
CHOLESTEROL	8mg	RIBOFLAVIN	*
SODIUM	110mg	NIACIN	2%
POTASSIUM	25mg	CALCIUM	2%
		IRON	2%

*Contains less than 2% of the U.S. RDA of this nutrient.

Cherry-Poppy Seed Twinks

The cream cheese in this cookie combines wonderfully with the orange and carrot flavors to make a rich, cake-like cookie.

Frosted Orange-Carrot Cookies

COOKIES
- 1 cup sugar
- ½ cup margarine or butter, softened
- 3-oz. pkg. cream cheese, softened
- 1 egg
- 2 teaspoons grated orange peel
- 1 cup (2 medium) shredded carrots
- 2 cups Pillsbury's BEST® All Purpose or Unbleached Flour
- ½ teaspoon baking soda
- ½ teaspoon cinnamon
- ¼ teaspoon nutmeg
- ¼ teaspoon salt

FROSTING
- 1¾ cups powdered sugar
- ¼ cup margarine or butter, softened
- 1 teaspoon grated orange peel
- 2 to 3 tablespoons orange juice

Heat oven to 350°F. Lightly grease cookie sheets. In large bowl, beat sugar, ½ cup margarine and cream cheese until light and fluffy. Add egg and orange peel; blend well. Stir in carrots. Lightly spoon flour into measuring cup; level off. Stir in flour, baking soda, cinnamon, nutmeg and salt; mix well. Drop by rounded teaspoonfuls 2 inches apart onto prepared cookie sheets. Bake at 350°F. for 10 to 12 minutes or until edges are light golden brown. Immediately remove from cookie sheets. Cool completely.

In small bowl, blend all frosting ingredients, adding enough orange juice for desired spreading consistency. Frost cooled cookies. 3 dozen cookies.

HIGH ALTITUDE—Above 3500 Feet: No change.

NUTRITION INFORMATION PER SERVING

SERVING SIZE: 1 COOKIE		PERCENT U.S. RDA PER SERVING	
CALORIES	110	PROTEIN	*
PROTEIN	1g	VITAMIN A	20%
CARBOHYDRATE	16g	VITAMIN C	*
FAT	5g	THIAMINE	2%
CHOLESTEROL	10mg	RIBOFLAVIN	*
SODIUM	85mg	NIACIN	2%
POTASSIUM	30mg	CALCIUM	2%
		IRON	2%

*Contains less than 2% of the U.S. RDA of this nutrient.

Frosted Orange-Carrot Cookies
Frosted Cherry Drops

This rich, soft, cherry cookie is a real eye catcher and is quick to mix. A 10-ounce jar of maraschino cherries will be enough for the entire batch of cookies.

Frosted Cherry Drops

COOKIES
- 1 pkg. Pillsbury Plus White Cake Mix
- ½ cup dairy sour cream
- 3 tablespoons cherry juice or water
- ¼ teaspoon almond extract
- 1 egg
- ½ cup finely chopped maraschino cherries

FROSTING
- 2½ cups powdered sugar
- ¼ cup margarine or butter, softened
- 1 tablespoon cherry juice
- 2 to 3 tablespoons half-and-half or milk
  Maraschino cherries, cut into fourths

Heat oven to 350°F. In large bowl, combine cake mix, sour cream, 3 tablespoons cherry juice, almond extract and egg; stir until well blended. Fold in cherries. Drop by teaspoonfuls 2 inches apart onto ungreased cookie sheets. Bake at 350°F. for 8 to 12 minutes or until edges are light golden brown. Cool 1 minute; remove from cookie sheets. Cool completely.

In small bowl, combine all frosting ingredients except maraschino cherries, adding enough half-and-half for desired spreading consistency. Frost cooled cookies. Top each with one-fourth maraschino cherry.
2½ to 3 dozen cookies.

HIGH ALTITUDE—Above 3500 Feet: Add 3 tablespoons flour to dry cake mix. Bake as directed above.

NUTRITION INFORMATION PER SERVING

SERVING SIZE: 1 COOKIE		PERCENT U.S. RDA PER SERVING	
CALORIES	120	PROTEIN	*
PROTEIN	1g	VITAMIN A	*
CARBOHYDRATE	21g	VITAMIN C	*
FAT	4g	THIAMINE	2%
CHOLESTEROL	10mg	RIBOFLAVIN	*
SODIUM	115mg	NIACIN	*
POTASSIUM	25mg	CALCIUM	*
		IRON	*

*Contains less than 2% of the U.S. RDA of this nutrient.

These cookies are good with milk or coffee if you like to dunk. And yes, they can be served for breakfast. They are more nutritious than a sugared doughnut.

Breakfast Cookie Crunchies

1	cup firmly packed brown sugar
½	cup margarine or butter, softened
½	cup oil
2	teaspoons lemon juice
1	egg
1½	cups Pillsbury's BEST® All Purpose or Unbleached Flour
½	teaspoon cream of tartar
½	teaspoon baking soda
¼	teaspoon salt
¼	teaspoon allspice
1	cup crisp rice cereal
½	cup rolled oats
¼	cup wheat germ

Heat oven to 350°F. In large bowl, beat brown sugar, margarine, oil and lemon juice until light and fluffy. Add egg; blend well. Lightly spoon flour into measuring cup; level off. Stir in flour, cream of tartar, baking soda, salt and allspice; mix well. Stir in rice cereal, oats and wheat germ. Drop by tablespoonfuls onto ungreased cookie sheets. Bake at 350°F. for 10 to 12 minutes or until light golden brown. Cool 1 minute; remove from cookie sheets. 2½ to 3 dozen cookies.

HIGH ALTITUDE—Above 3500 Feet: No change.

NUTRITION INFORMATION PER SERVING

SERVING SIZE: 1 COOKIE		PERCENT U.S. RDA PER SERVING	
CALORIES	100	PROTEIN	*
PROTEIN	1g	VITAMIN A	2%
CARBOHYDRATE	12g	VITAMIN C	*
FAT	6g	THIAMINE	4%
CHOLESTEROL	8mg	RIBOFLAVIN	2%
SODIUM	70mg	NIACIN	2%
POTASSIUM	40mg	CALCIUM	*
		IRON	2%

*Contains less than 2% of the U.S. RDA of this nutrient.

Deliciously tempting peanut butter cookies with an interesting combination of peanuts and butterscotch chips.

Double Peanut Scotchies

¾	cup firmly packed brown sugar
½	cup margarine or butter, softened
½	cup peanut butter
2	eggs
1½	cups Pillsbury's BEST® All Purpose or Unbleached Flour
1	teaspoon baking soda
1	cup peanuts
6-oz.	pkg. (1 cup) butterscotch chips

Heat oven to 350°F. In large bowl, beat brown sugar and margarine until light and fluffy. Add peanut butter and eggs; blend well. Lightly spoon flour into measuring cup; level off. Stir in flour and baking soda; mix well. Stir in peanuts and butterscotch chips. Drop by rounded teaspoonfuls 2 inches apart onto ungreased cookie sheets. Bake at 350°F. for 9 to 12 minutes or until golden brown. Immediately remove from cookie sheets. 4 dozen cookies.

HIGH ALTITUDE—Above 3500 Feet: No change.

NUTRITION INFORMATION PER SERVING

SERVING SIZE: 1 COOKIE		PERCENT U.S. RDA PER SERVING	
CALORIES	100	PROTEIN	2%
PROTEIN	2g	VITAMIN A	*
CARBOHYDRATE	9g	VITAMIN C	*
FAT	6g	THIAMINE	2%
CHOLESTEROL	10mg	RIBOFLAVIN	*
SODIUM	60mg	NIACIN	4%
POTASSIUM	60mg	CALCIUM	*
		IRON	2%

*Contains less than 2% of the U.S. RDA of this nutrient.

A large, soft-textured cookie with a mild pumpkin flavor and candy-coated, chocolate-covered peanuts dispersed throughout.

Pumpkin Candy Cookies

½ cup sugar
½ cup firmly packed brown sugar
1 cup margarine or butter, softened
1 teaspoon vanilla
1 egg
1 cup canned or smoothly mashed, cooked pumpkin
2 cups Pillsbury's BEST® All Purpose or Unbleached Flour
1 teaspoon baking soda
½ teaspoon salt
1½ teaspoons cinnamon
½ teaspoon ginger
1 cup candy-coated chocolate-covered peanuts

Heat oven to 350ºF. In large bowl, beat sugar, brown sugar and margarine until light and fluffy. Add vanilla, egg and pumpkin; blend well. Lightly spoon flour into measuring cup; level off. Stir in flour, baking soda, salt, cinnamon and ginger; mix well. Stir in candy. Drop by rounded tablespoonfuls 3 inches apart onto ungreased cookie sheets. Using metal spoon, flatten into 3-inch circles. Bake at 350ºF. for 14 to 17 minutes or until edges are light golden brown. Cool 1 minute; remove from cookie sheets.
2 dozen cookies.

HIGH ALTITUDE—Above 3500 Feet: No change.

NUTRITION INFORMATION PER SERVING

SERVING SIZE: 1 COOKIE		PERCENT U.S. RDA PER SERVING	
CALORIES	200	PROTEIN	4%
PROTEIN	3g	VITAMIN A	25%
CARBOHYDRATE	22g	VITAMIN C	*
FAT	11g	THIAMINE	6%
CHOLESTEROL	10mg	RIBOFLAVIN	4%
SODIUM	210mg	NIACIN	6%
POTASSIUM	85mg	CALCIUM	4%
		IRON	4%

*Contains less than 2% of the U.S. RDA of this nutrient.

A blend of familiar spices—cinnamon, allspice, cardamom, ginger and nutmeg —makes this a memorable cookie.

Five Spice Apple Cookies

¾ cup sugar
¾ cup firmly packed brown sugar
1 cup margarine or butter, softened
1 teaspoon vanilla
2 eggs
2 cups Pillsbury's BEST® All Purpose or Unbleached Flour
1 teaspoon baking soda
1 teaspoon salt
1 teaspoon cinnamon
¼ teaspoon allspice
¼ teaspoon cardamom
¼ teaspoon ginger
¼ teaspoon nutmeg
2 cups rolled oats
1 cup (1 medium) shredded apple

Heat oven to 375ºF. Lightly grease cookie sheets. In large bowl, beat sugar, brown sugar and margarine until light and fluffy. Add vanilla and eggs; blend well. Lightly spoon flour into measuring cup; level off. Stir in flour, baking soda, salt, cinnamon, allspice, cardamom, ginger and nutmeg; mix well. Stir in oats and apple. Drop by rounded teaspoonfuls 2 inches apart onto prepared cookie sheets. Bake at 375ºF. for 9 to 11 minutes or until light golden brown. Cool 1 minute; remove from cookie sheets.
4 dozen cookies.

HIGH ALTITUDE—Above 3500 Feet: No change.

NUTRITION INFORMATION PER SERVING

SERVING SIZE: 1 COOKIE		PERCENT U.S. RDA PER SERVING	
CALORIES	100	PROTEIN	2%
PROTEIN	1g	VITAMIN A	2%
CARBOHYDRATE	13g	VITAMIN C	*
FAT	4g	THIAMINE	4%
CHOLESTEROL	10mg	RIBOFLAVIN	*
SODIUM	115mg	NIACIN	*
POTASSIUM	40mg	CALCIUM	*
		IRON	2%

*Contains less than 2% of the U.S. RDA of this nutrient.

A wonderful "homemade" cookie from a mix that is ideal for children to prepare.

Peanut Butter Autumn Spotlights

1 pkg. Pillsbury Plus Yellow Cake Mix
½ cup peanut butter
¼ cup margarine or butter, softened
¼ cup water
2 eggs
1 cup candy coated peanut butter pieces

Heat oven to 350°F. In large bowl, combine cake mix, peanut butter, margarine, water and eggs; stir until well blended. Fold in candy pieces. Drop by rounded teaspoonfuls 2 inches apart onto ungreased cookie sheets. Bake at 350°F. for 8 to 12 minutes or until light golden brown. Immediately remove from cookie sheets. 3½ dozen cookies.

HIGH ALTITUDE—Above 3500 Feet: Add 3 tablespoons flour to dry cake mix. Bake as directed above.

NUTRITION INFORMATION PER SERVING

SERVING SIZE: 1 COOKIE		PERCENT U.S. RDA PER SERVING	
CALORIES	100	PROTEIN	2%
PROTEIN	2g	VITAMIN A	*
CARBOHYDRATE	13g	VITAMIN C	*
FAT	5g	THIAMINE	2%
CHOLESTEROL	10mg	RIBOFLAVIN	2%
SODIUM	115mg	NIACIN	4%
POTASSIUM	40mg	CALCIUM	*
		IRON	2%

*Contains less than 2% of the U.S. RDA of this nutrient.

Peanut Butter Autumn Spotlights

A new twist to a coconut macaroon that is moist and chewy.

Raisin Macaroons

4 eggs, separated
¼ teaspoon salt
1½ cups sugar
3 cups coconut
1½ cups Pillsbury's BEST® All Purpose or Unbleached Flour
1½ cups raisins
1 to 2 teaspoons coconut extract

Heat oven to 350ºF. Grease cookie sheets. In small bowl, beat egg whites and salt until foamy. Gradually add sugar; beat until stiff peaks form, about 4 minutes. In large bowl, slightly beat egg yolks; stir in coconut. Lightly spoon flour into measuring cup; level off. Stir in flour, raisins and coconut extract; mix well. By hand, fold in egg whites. Drop by rounded teaspoonfuls 2 inches apart onto prepared cookie sheets. Bake at 350ºF. for 10 to 15 minutes or until set and edges are very light golden brown. 5 dozen cookies.

HIGH ALTITUDE—Above 3500 Feet: No change.

NUTRITION INFORMATION PER SERVING

SERVING SIZE: 1 COOKIE		PERCENT U.S. RDA PER SERVING	
CALORIES	70	PROTEIN	*
PROTEIN	1g	VITAMIN A	*
CARBOHYDRATE	12g	VITAMIN C	*
FAT	2g	THIAMINE	2%
CHOLESTEROL	20mg	RIBOFLAVIN	*
SODIUM	15mg	NIACIN	*
POTASSIUM	50mg	CALCIUM	*
		IRON	2%

*Contains less than 2% of the U.S. RDA of this nutrient.

A sour cream chocolate cookie filled with dried fruit and nuts.

Chocolate Fruit-Nut Cookies

½ cup firmly packed brown sugar
¼ cup sugar
¼ cup margarine or butter, softened
⅔ cup dairy sour cream
2 oz. (2 squares) unsweetened chocolate, melted, cooled
2 tablespoons water
1 teaspoon vanilla
1 egg
1½ cups Pillsbury's BEST® All Purpose or Unbleached Flour
½ teaspoon baking soda
½ teaspoon cinnamon
¼ teaspoon salt
6-oz. pkg. dried fruit bits
1 to 1½ cups coarsely chopped nuts

Heat oven to 350ºF. Grease cookie sheets. In large bowl, beat brown sugar, sugar and margarine until light and fluffy. Add sour cream, chocolate, water, vanilla and egg; blend well. Lightly spoon flour into measuring cup; level off. Stir in flour, baking soda, cinnamon and salt; mix well. Stir in fruit bits and nuts. Drop by rounded teaspoonfuls onto prepared cookie sheets. Bake at 350ºF. for 8 to 12 minutes or until set. Immediately remove from cookie sheets. 4 dozen cookies.

HIGH ALTITUDE—Above 3500 Feet: No change.

NUTRITION INFORMATION PER SERVING

SERVING SIZE: 1 COOKIE		PERCENT U.S. RDA PER SERVING	
CALORIES	90	PROTEIN	2%
PROTEIN	1g	VITAMIN A	4%
CARBOHYDRATE	10g	VITAMIN C	*
FAT	5g	THIAMINE	2%
CHOLESTEROL	6mg	RIBOFLAVIN	2%
SODIUM	40mg	NIACIN	*
POTASSIUM	80mg	CALCIUM	2%
		IRON	2%

*Contains less than 2% of the U.S. RDA of this nutrient.

Get out a bowl and spoon and in no time a soft, walnut-packed cookie can be yours. Try decorator sprinkles, colored sugar or candied cherries as an alternative to the walnut garnish.

Walnut Quickie Drops

1	pkg. Pillsbury Plus Butter Recipe Cake Mix
8-oz.	carton vanilla yogurt
1	egg, slightly beaten
2	tablespoons margarine or butter, melted
1	cup finely chopped walnuts
36	walnut halves or pieces, if desired

Heat oven to 350°F. In large bowl, combine all ingredients except walnut halves; stir until well blended. Drop by teaspoonfuls 2 inches apart onto ungreased cookie sheets. Press walnut halves in center of each cookie. Bake at 350°F. for 11 to 14 minutes or until set. Cool 1 minute; remove from cookie sheets. Cool completely. Store in loosely covered container. 3 dozen cookies.

HIGH ALTITUDE—Above 3500 Feet: No change.

NUTRITION INFORMATION PER SERVING

SERVING SIZE: 1 COOKIE		PERCENT U.S. RDA PER SERVING	
CALORIES	100	PROTEIN	2%
PROTEIN	2g	VITAMIN A	*
CARBOHYDRATE	13g	VITAMIN C	*
FAT	5g	THIAMINE	2%
CHOLESTEROL	8mg	RIBOFLAVIN	*
SODIUM	80mg	NIACIN	*
POTASSIUM	45mg	CALCIUM	2%
		IRON	2%

*Contains less than 2% of the U.S. RDA of this nutrient.

Fun-loving kids of all ages will enjoy these crunchy treats filled with their favorite candies.

White Chocolate Bird Nests

2	cups chow mein noodles
2	cups cornflakes cereal, coarsely crushed
1	lb. white chocolate or vanilla-flavored candy coating, cut into pieces
⅓	cup fruit flavored pectin candies, chocolate covered raisins or candy-coated chocolate pieces

Place sheet of waxed paper on large cookie sheet. In large bowl, combine noodles and cereal; set aside. In double boiler over hot water, melt chocolate. Remove from heat; pour over noodles and cereal. To form nests, mound 2 tablespoons of mixture onto prepared cookie sheet. Make indentation in center of each mound; press 3 candies in center. Allow to set at room temperature until firm. 18 cookies.

◼ MICROWAVE DIRECTIONS: Place chocolate in 8-cup microwave-safe measuring cup or bowl. Microwave on MEDIUM 5 to 6 minutes or until melted, stirring twice. Continue as directed above.

NUTRITION INFORMATION PER SERVING

SERVING SIZE: 1 COOKIE		PERCENT U.S. RDA PER SERVING	
CALORIES	190	PROTEIN	2%
PROTEIN	2g	VITAMIN A	2%
CARBOHYDRATE	25g	VITAMIN C	2%
FAT	10g	THIAMINE	2%
CHOLESTEROL	0mg	RIBOFLAVIN	2%
SODIUM	80mg	NIACIN	2%
POTASSIUM	90mg	CALCIUM	*
		IRON	4%

*Contains less than 2% of the U.S. RDA of this nutrient.

This cookie, flavored with molasses and spices, is crunchy on the edges and chewy on the inside.

Molasses Crunchies

¾ cup sugar
½ cup margarine or butter, softened
¼ cup light molasses
1 teaspoon vanilla
1 egg
1½ cups Pillsbury's BEST® All Purpose or Unbleached Flour
½ teaspoon baking soda
½ teaspoon cinnamon
¼ teaspoon nutmeg
⅛ teaspoon allspice
3 cups cereal flakes with raisins and almonds

Heat oven to 350°F. Lightly grease cookie sheets. In large bowl, beat sugar and margarine until light and fluffy. Add molasses, vanilla and egg; blend well. Lightly spoon flour into measuring cup; level off. Stir in flour, baking soda, cinnamon, nutmeg and allspice; mix well. Fold in cereal. Drop by rounded teaspoonfuls 2 inches apart onto prepared cookie sheets. Bake at 350°F. for 8 to 12 minutes or until light golden brown. Immediately remove from cookie sheets. 3 dozen cookies.

HIGH ALTITUDE—Above 3500 Feet: Increase flour to 1½ cups plus 2 tablespoons. Bake as directed above.

NUTRITION INFORMATION PER SERVING

SERVING SIZE: 1 COOKIE		PERCENT U.S. RDA PER SERVING	
CALORIES	80	PROTEIN	*
PROTEIN	1g	VITAMIN A	2%
CARBOHYDRATE	13g	VITAMIN C	*
FAT	3g	THIAMINE	2%
CHOLESTEROL	8mg	RIBOFLAVIN	*
SODIUM	55mg	NIACIN	*
POTASSIUM	50mg	CALCIUM	2%
		IRON	2%

*Contains less than 2% of the U.S. RDA of this nutrient.

If you think a cookie with a wholesome blend of ingredients can't please the sweet tooth, you've got to try this recipe.

Whole Wheat Zucchini Cookies

¾ cup sugar
¾ cup firmly packed brown sugar
1 cup margarine or butter, softened
1 teaspoon vanilla
1 teaspoon grated lemon peel
2 eggs
2½ cups Pillsbury's BEST® Whole Wheat Flour
1 teaspoon baking soda
1 teaspoon cinnamon
½ teaspoon salt
2 cups quick-cooking rolled oats
2 cups shredded zucchini, drained
12-oz. pkg. (2 cups) miniature semi-sweet chocolate chips

Heat oven to 350°F. Lightly grease cookie sheets. In large bowl, beat sugar, brown sugar and margarine until light and fluffy. Add vanilla, lemon peel and eggs; blend well. Lightly spoon flour into measuring cup; level off. Stir in whole wheat flour, baking soda, cinnamon and salt; mix well. Stir in oats, zucchini and chocolate chips. Drop by rounded teaspoonfuls onto prepared cookie sheets. Bake at 350°F. for 9 to 13 minutes or until golden brown. Immediately remove from cookie sheets; cool completely. Store loosely covered. 5 dozen cookies.

HIGH ALTITUDE—Above 3500 Feet: No change.

NUTRITION INFORMATION PER SERVING

SERVING SIZE: 1 COOKIE		PERCENT U.S. RDA PER SERVING	
CALORIES	110	PROTEIN	2%
PROTEIN	2g	VITAMIN A	2%
CARBOHYDRATE	14g	VITAMIN C	*
FAT	6g	THIAMINE	2%
CHOLESTEROL	8mg	RIBOFLAVIN	*
SODIUM	75mg	NIACIN	*
POTASSIUM	65mg	CALCIUM	*
		IRON	2%

*Contains less than 2% of the U.S. RDA of this nutrient.

A sparkling sugar glaze makes these tart and tangy lemonade drop cookies look special.

Lemonade Drops

1 cup sugar
½ cup margarine or butter, softened
½ cup shortening
2 eggs
3 cups Pillsbury's BEST® All Purpose or Unbleached Flour
1 teaspoon baking soda
½ teaspoon salt
6-oz. can frozen lemonade concentrate, thawed, reserving 3 tablespoons
Sugar

Heat oven to 375°F. Lightly grease cookie sheets. In large bowl, combine sugar, margarine, shortening and eggs; beat well. Lightly spoon flour into measuring cup; level off. In small bowl, combine flour, soda and salt. Alternately add dry ingredients and lemonade concentrate to sugar mixture, mixing well after each addition. Drop by teaspoonfuls onto prepared cookie sheets. Bake at 375°F. for 8 to 10 minutes or until lightly browned. Remove from cookie sheets; place on wire racks. Brush with reserved lemonade concentrate; sprinkle lightly with sugar. Cool. 5 dozen cookies.

HIGH ALTITUDE—Above 3500 Feet: No change.

NUTRITION INFORMATION PER SERVING

SERVING SIZE: 1 COOKIE		PERCENT U.S. RDA PER SERVING	
CALORIES	70	PROTEIN	*
PROTEIN	1g	VITAMIN A	*
CARBOHYDRATE	10g	VITAMIN C	*
FAT	3g	THIAMINE	2%
CHOLESTEROL	8mg	RIBOFLAVIN	*
SODIUM	55mg	NIACIN	*
POTASSIUM	15mg	CALCIUM	*
		IRON	*

*Contains less than 2% of the U.S. RDA of this nutrient.

A chewy, deliciously nutritious cookie that stores and travels well.

Apricot Oatmeal Drops

¾ cup firmly packed brown sugar
½ cup margarine or butter, softened
3 tablespoons water
1 teaspoon vanilla
1 egg
2 cups quick-cooking rolled oats
¾ cup Pillsbury's BEST® All Purpose or Unbleached Flour
1 teaspoon baking soda
¼ teaspoon salt
½ cup chopped dried apricots
½ cup chopped nuts

Heat oven to 325°F. Lightly grease cookie sheets. In large bowl, beat brown sugar and margarine until light and fluffy. Add water, vanilla and egg; blend well. Lightly spoon flour into measuring cup; level off. Stir in oats, flour, baking soda and salt; mix well. Fold in apricots and nuts. Drop by rounded teaspoonfuls onto prepared cookie sheets. Bake at 325°F. for 10 to 15 minutes or until edges are light golden brown. Immediately remove from cookie sheets. 2½ dozen cookies.

HIGH ALTITUDE—Above 3500 Feet: No change.

NUTRITION INFORMATION PER SERVING

SERVING SIZE: 1 COOKIE		PERCENT U.S. RDA PER SERVING	
CALORIES	100	PROTEIN	2%
PROTEIN	2g	VITAMIN A	6%
CARBOHYDRATE	13g	VITAMIN C	*
FAT	5g	THIAMINE	4%
CHOLESTEROL	8mg	RIBOFLAVIN	*
SODIUM	95mg	NIACIN	*
POTASSIUM	85mg	CALCIUM	*
		IRON	4%

*Contains less than 2% of the U.S. RDA of this nutrient.

Big Batch
BONANZA

Big Batch
BONANZA

When more makes sense...

When it's time to bake and all ingredients and utensils are in readiness, it often makes sense to bake a time-saving batch. Extra cookies mean extra enjoyment when there is an abundance for the cookie jar, to share with a neighbor or to mail to someone special who is far from home cooking. And, extra cookies can be frozen to quickly replenish that cookie jar or to freeze ahead for a carefree holiday season. As you watch that big batch vanish, there is no doubt that your baking efforts are appreciated!

When mailing cookies, you have two tasks —to seal out drying air and to protect the contents with plenty of cushioning materials. When several kinds of goodies are mailed, wrap each type separately. Layer in a sturdy box, adding cushioning material as you go. Seal the box tightly with mailing tape and overwrap with strong mailing paper. Label clearly, mark the package "perishable" and consult the post office for the best method of posting.

Another big bonus for big batch baking is our recipes for refrigerating or freezing cookie dough for quick freshly-baked treats another day. Wrap the dough securely to seal out moisture and air and freeze up to six months. For an additional bonus, microwave directions are given for Slice 'N Bake Peanut Butter Cookies and Nut-Edged Lemon Cookie Slices. What could be easier than to slice and bake a few cookies at a time for warm-from-the-microwave oven goodness!

This crisp cookie with chopped hazelnuts and a hint of orange will make a hit at any gathering. Hazelnuts are also known as filberts.

Centerstage Hazelnut Cookies

1 cup sugar
1 cup powdered sugar
1 cup margarine or butter, softened
1 cup oil
1 teaspoon vanilla
2 teaspoons grated orange peel
2 eggs
4¼ cups Pillsbury's BEST® All Purpose or Unbleached Flour
1 teaspoon baking soda
1 teaspoon cream of tartar
1 teaspoon salt
½ teaspoon nutmeg or mace
1 cup chopped hazelnuts (filberts)
Sugar
Hazelnut halves or pieces of candied cherry for garnish, if desired

In large bowl, beat sugar, powdered sugar, margarine, oil, vanilla, orange peel and eggs until well blended. Lightly spoon flour into measuring cup; level off. Stir in flour, baking soda, cream of tartar, salt and nutmeg; mix well. Stir in nuts. Cover with plastic wrap; refrigerate at least 2 hours or overnight.

Heat oven to 375°F. Shape dough into 1-inch balls; roll in sugar. Place 2 inches apart on ungreased cookie sheets. Flatten with bottom of glass dipped in sugar. Top with hazelnut half. Bake at 375°F. for 7 to 10 minutes or until set. 8 dozen cookies.

HIGH ALTITUDE—Above 3500 Feet: No change.

NUTRITION INFORMATION PER SERVING

SERVING SIZE: 1 COOKIE		PERCENT U.S. RDA PER SERVING	
CALORIES	80	PROTEIN	*
PROTEIN	1g	VITAMIN A	*
CARBOHYDRATE	8g	VITAMIN C	*
FAT	5g	THIAMINE	2%
CHOLESTEROL	6mg	RIBOFLAVIN	*
SODIUM	55mg	NIACIN	*
POTASSIUM	15mg	CALCIUM	*
		IRON	*

*Contains less than 2% of the U.S. RDA of this nutrient.

Shown on pages 20 and 21 —
L to R: Soft and Chewy Granola Cookies pg.23, Slice 'N Bake Peanut Butter Cookies pg.26, Centerstage Hazelnut Cookies pg.23

A sure-to-please, hearty cookie! Store between sheets of waxed paper in a tightly covered container. Store baked cookies for up to 6 months in freezer.

Soft and Chewy Granola Cookies

3 cups rolled oats
1½ cups Pillsbury's BEST® All Purpose or Unbleached Flour
1 cup wheat germ
1 teaspoon baking powder
½ teaspoon salt
1 cup firmly packed brown sugar
1 cup margarine or butter, softened
½ cup honey
1½ teaspoons vanilla
2 eggs
½ cup raisins
½ cup chopped almonds
¼ cup sesame seeds
¼ cup sunflower nuts

Heat oven to 375°F. Lightly grease cookie sheets. Lightly spoon flour into measuring cup; level off. In medium bowl, combine oats, flour, wheat germ, baking powder and salt; mix well. Set aside. In large bowl, beat brown sugar, margarine and honey until light and fluffy. Add vanilla and eggs; blend well. Stir in flour mixture. Add raisins, almonds, sesame seeds and sunflower nuts; mix well. Drop by rounded teaspoonfuls onto prepared cookie sheets. Bake at 375°F. for 7 to 8 minutes or until edges are light golden brown. Immediately remove from cookie sheets. 5 dozen cookies.

TIP: For large sized cookies, place ¼ cup of dough 4 inches apart on prepared cookie sheets. Using metal spoon, flatten into 3-inch circles. Bake at 375°F. for 12 to 14 minutes.

HIGH ALTITUDE—Above 3500 Feet: No change.

NUTRITION INFORMATION PER SERVING

SERVING SIZE: 1 COOKIE		PERCENT U.S. RDA PER SERVING	
CALORIES	100	PROTEIN	2%
PROTEIN	2g	VITAMIN A	2%
CARBOHYDRATE	13g	VITAMIN C	*
FAT	5g	THIAMINE	6%
CHOLESTEROL	8mg	RIBOFLAVIN	2%
SODIUM	60mg	NIACIN	*
POTASSIUM	70mg	CALCIUM	2%
		IRON	4%

*Contains less than 2% of the U.S. RDA of this nutrient.

Chocolate lovers will find this eye-catching version of a cookie classic irresistible. Smaller-sized snaps can be made for upcoming holiday cookie trays.

Crisp Chocolate Snaps

    2 cups sugar
    1 cup firmly packed brown sugar
 1 ½ cups margarine or butter,
         softened
    2 teaspoons vanilla
    3 eggs
    6 oz. (6 squares) unsweetened
         chocolate, melted, cooled
   ½ teaspoon red food coloring, if
         desired
    4 cups Pillsbury's BEST® All
         Purpose or Unbleached Flour
    2 teaspoons baking soda
    1 teaspoon salt
       Sugar

Heat oven to 350°F. Lightly grease cookie sheets. In large bowl, beat sugar, brown sugar and margarine until light and fluffy. Add vanilla, eggs, unsweetened chocolate and food coloring; blend well. Lightly spoon flour into measuring cup; level off. Stir in flour, baking soda and salt; mix well. If necessary, refrigerate up to 24 hours for easier handling.

Shape dough into 1 ½-inch balls; roll in sugar. Place 3 inches apart on prepared cookie sheets. Bake at 350°F. for 8 to 12 minutes or until set. (Cookies will puff up and flatten during baking.) Cool 1 minute; remove from cookie sheets. 6 dozen cookies.

HIGH ALTITUDE—Above 3500 Feet: No change.

NUTRITION INFORMATION PER SERVING

SERVING SIZE: 1 COOKIE		PERCENT U.S. RDA PER SERVING	
CALORIES	110	PROTEIN	*
PROTEIN	1g	VITAMIN A	2%
CARBOHYDRATE	15g	VITAMIN C	*
FAT	5g	THIAMINE	2%
CHOLESTEROL	10mg	RIBOFLAVIN	2%
SODIUM	110mg	NIACIN	2%
POTASSIUM	45mg	CALCIUM	2%
		IRON	2%

*Contains less than 2% of the U.S. RDA of this nutrient.

On the theory that one can't have too much of a good thing, here is a recipe for 10 dozen flavorful ginger cookies. Store tightly covered at room temperature or for up to 6 months in the freezer.

Ginger Cookies

    2 cups sugar
 1 ½ cups margarine or butter,
         softened
   ½ cup molasses
    2 eggs
 4 ½ cups Pillsbury's BEST® All
         Purpose or Unbleached Flour
    3 teaspoons baking soda
   ½ teaspoon salt
    2 teaspoons cinnamon
    1 teaspoon cloves
    1 teaspoon ginger
   ½ teaspoon nutmeg
       Sugar

In large bowl, beat sugar, margarine, molasses and eggs until light and fluffy. Lightly spoon flour into measuring cup; level off. Stir in flour, baking soda, salt, cinnamon, cloves, ginger and nutmeg; mix well. Cover with plastic wrap; refrigerate 1 hour.

Heat oven to 350°F. Shape dough into 1-inch balls; roll in sugar. Place 2 inches apart on ungreased cookie sheets. Bake at 350°F. for 8 to 12 minutes or until set. (Cookies will puff up and flatten during baking.) Cool 1 minute; remove from cookie sheets. 10 dozen cookies.

HIGH ALTITUDE—Above 3500 Feet: No change.

NUTRITION INFORMATION PER SERVING

SERVING SIZE: 1 COOKIE		PERCENT U.S. RDA PER SERVING	
CALORIES	50	PROTEIN	*
PROTEIN	1g	VITAMIN A	*
CARBOHYDRATE	8g	VITAMIN C	*
FAT	2g	THIAMINE	2%
CHOLESTEROL	4mg	RIBOFLAVIN	*
SODIUM	65mg	NIACIN	*
POTASSIUM	25mg	CALCIUM	*
		IRON	*

*Contains less than 2% of the U.S. RDA of this nutrient.

Crisp Chocolate Snaps
Ginger Cookies

This updated version of Grandma's icebox cookies combines oatmeal and wheat germ for a textured cookie with a pleasing peanut butter and coconut flavor. Store in the freezer and microwave a few at a time.

Slice 'N Bake Peanut Butter Cookies

1 ¾ cups firmly packed brown
    sugar
  1 cup peanut butter
  ¾ cup margarine or butter,
    softened
  1 teaspoon vanilla
  2 eggs
  2 cups Pillsbury's BEST® All
    Purpose or Unbleached Flour
  1 teaspoon baking powder
  ½ teaspoon baking soda
  ½ teaspoon salt
  1 cup coconut
  ¾ cup wheat germ
  ½ cup rolled oats

In large bowl, beat sugar, peanut butter and margarine until light and fluffy. Add vanilla and eggs; blend well. Lightly spoon flour into measuring cup; level off. Stir in flour, baking powder, baking soda and salt; mix well. Stir in coconut, wheat germ and oats. Divide dough in half. On waxed paper, shape each half into 2x1½-inch rectangular rolls; wrap and freeze overnight or until firm.

Heat oven to 375ºF. Cut dough into ¼-inch slices. Place 1 inch apart on ungreased cookie sheets. Bake at 375ºF. for 8 to 10 minutes or until edges are light golden brown. Cool 1 minute; remove from cookie sheets. 5 dozen cookies.

TIP: Cookie dough may be wrapped in foil and stored in freezer up to 6 weeks.

■▌ MICROWAVE DIRECTIONS:
Prepare cookie dough as directed above. Lightly grease inverted 9-inch round or square microwave-safe dish. Place 6 dough slices in spoke fashion, spacing evenly apart. Microwave on HIGH for 2¼ to 3 minutes or until no fingerprint remains when lightly touched with finger, rotating dish once halfway through cooking. Cool 1 minute; remove from baking dish.

TIP: A microwave-safe baking sheet or microwave-safe pizza dish may be substituted for inverted 9-inch microwave-safe dish.

HIGH ALTITUDE—Above 3500 Feet: No change.

NUTRITION INFORMATION PER SERVING

SERVING SIZE: 1 COOKIE		PERCENT U.S. RDA PER SERVING	
CALORIES	100	PROTEIN	2%
PROTEIN	2g	VITAMIN A	2%
CARBOHYDRATE	12g	VITAMIN C	*
FAT	5g	THIAMINE	4%
CHOLESTEROL	8mg	RIBOFLAVIN	*
SODIUM	85mg	NIACIN	4%
POTASSIUM	75mg	CALCIUM	2%
		IRON	4%

*Contains less than 2% of the U.S. RDA of this nutrient.

A popular totable bar for school lunches, office coffee breaks and bedtime snacks.

Chewy Cereal Squares

  5 cups cornflakes cereal
  3 cups crisp rice cereal
  1 cup salted peanuts
  1 cup coconut
  ½ cup margarine or butter
  1 cup sugar
  1 cup light corn syrup
  ½ cup half-and-half

Butter 15x10-inch jelly roll pan. In large bowl, combine cereals, peanuts and coconut. In medium saucepan, melt margarine; stir in sugar, corn syrup and half-and-half. Cook over medium heat, stirring occasionally, until candy thermometer reaches soft ball stage (234ºF.). Pour over cereal mixture; toss until well coated. Spread in prepared pan. Cool completely; cut into squares. 36 squares.

NUTRITION INFORMATION PER SERVING

SERVING SIZE: 1 SQUARE		PERCENT U.S. RDA PER SERVING	
CALORIES	130	PROTEIN	2%
PROTEIN	2g	VITAMIN A	6%
CARBOHYDRATE	19g	VITAMIN C	2%
FAT	6g	THIAMINE	6%
CHOLESTEROL	0mg	RIBOFLAVIN	4%
SODIUM	120mg	NIACIN	8%
POTASSIUM	45mg	CALCIUM	*
		IRON	4%

*Contains less than 2% of the U.S. RDA of this nutrient.

Dates have always been recognized as a good high-energy food because of their carbohydrate, iron and protein content. Store dates tightly covered at room temperature or in the refrigerator for longer storage.

Chewy Date Drops

      2 cups chopped dates
    ½ cup sugar
    ½ cup water
      1 cup firmly packed brown sugar
    ½ cup sugar
      1 cup margarine or butter,
          softened
      1 teaspoon vanilla
      3 eggs
      4 cups Pillsbury's BEST® All
          Purpose or Unbleached Flour
      1 teaspoon baking soda
      1 teaspoon salt
      1 cup chopped walnuts

In medium saucepan, combine dates, ½ cup sugar and water. Cook over medium heat until thickened, stirring occasionally. Cool.

Heat oven to 375°F. Grease cookie sheets. In large bowl, beat brown sugar, ½ cup sugar and margarine until light and fluffy. Add vanilla and eggs; blend well. Lightly spoon flour into measuring cup; level off. Stir in flour, baking soda and salt; mix well. Stir in date mixture and nuts. Drop by rounded teaspoonfuls 2 inches apart onto prepared cookie sheets. Bake at 375°F. for 8 to 10 minutes or until light golden brown. Immediately remove from cookie sheets. 6 dozen cookies.

HIGH ALTITUDE—Above 3500 Feet: Decrease sugar beaten with margarine to ¼ cup. Bake as directed above.

NUTRITION INFORMATION PER SERVING

SERVING SIZE: 1 COOKIE		PERCENT U.S. RDA PER SERVING	
CALORIES	100	PROTEIN	*
PROTEIN	1g	VITAMIN A	2%
CARBOHYDRATE	15g	VITAMIN C	*
FAT	4g	THIAMINE	4%
CHOLESTEROL	10mg	RIBOFLAVIN	2%
SODIUM	80mg	NIACIN	2%
POTASSIUM	65mg	CALCIUM	2%
		IRON	2%

*Contains less than 2% of the U.S. RDA of this nutrient.

A quick, simple treat with a pleasing flavor blend from Bake-Off® Contest 26.

Almond Crescent Crispy Bars

8-oz. can Pillsbury Refrigerated
          Quick Crescent Dinner
          Rolls
    ¼ to ½ teaspoon ginger
    ⅔ cup honey
      2 tablespoons butter or
          margarine, softened
    1 to 1½ teaspoons almond extract
      2 cups crisp rice cereal
    ½ to ¾ cup sliced almonds

Heat oven to 375°F. Unroll dough into two long rectangles. Place in ungreased 15x10-inch jelly roll pan; press over bottom to form crust. Seal perforations. In small bowl, blend ginger, honey, butter and almond extract; stir in cereal. Gently spread cereal mixture over dough; sprinkle nuts over filling. Bake at 375°F. for 11 to 13 minutes or until golden brown. Cool. Cut into bars. 48 bars.

NUTRITION INFORMATION PER SERVING

SERVING SIZE: 1 BAR		PERCENT U.S. RDA PER SERVING	
CALORIES	50	PROTEIN	*
PROTEIN	1g	VITAMIN A	*
CARBOHYDRATE	7g	VITAMIN C	*
FAT	2g	THIAMINE	2%
CHOLESTEROL	0mg	RIBOFLAVIN	2%
SODIUM	60mg	NIACIN	*
POTASSIUM	25mg	CALCIUM	*
		IRON	*

*Contains less than 2% of the U.S. RDA of this nutrient.

These moist fruit bars will delight a large gathering of friends.

Hummingbird Bars

BARS
- 3 cups Pillsbury's BEST® All Purpose or Unbleached Flour
- 2 cups sugar
- 1 teaspoon baking soda
- 1 teaspoon cinnamon
- ½ teaspoon salt
- 1 cup oil
- 2 teaspoons vanilla
- 2 cups (2 medium) diced bananas
- 1 cup chopped nuts
- 1 cup maraschino cherries, halved
- 3 eggs, slightly beaten
- 8-oz. can crushed pineapple, undrained

GLAZE
- ¼ cup butter or margarine, softened
- 1½ cups powdered sugar
- 1 to 2 tablespoons warm milk

Heat oven to 350ºF. Grease and flour 15x10x1-inch jelly roll pan. Lightly spoon flour into measuring cup; level off. In large bowl, combine all bar ingredients. Stir until blended. Spread evenly in prepared pan. Bake at 350ºF. for 30 to 40 minutes or until toothpick inserted in center comes out clean.

In small bowl, combine all glaze ingredients, adding enough milk for desired glaze consistency. Spread over warm bars. Cool completely; cut into bars. Store in refrigerator. 48 bars.

HIGH ALTITUDE—Above 3500 Feet: No change.

NUTRITION INFORMATION PER SERVING

SERVING SIZE: 1 BAR		PERCENT U.S. RDA PER SERVING	
CALORIES	150	PROTEIN	2%
PROTEIN	2g	VITAMIN A	*
CARBOHYDRATE	21g	VITAMIN C	*
FAT	7g	THIAMINE	4%
CHOLESTEROL	20mg	RIBOFLAVIN	2%
SODIUM	60mg	NIACIN	2%
POTASSIUM	60mg	CALCIUM	2%
		IRON	2%

*Contains less than 2% of the U.S. RDA of this nutrient.

Hummingbird Bars

This crunchy peanut butter and chocolate chip cookie stores and travels well.

Peanutty Chocolate Chippers

1 cup sugar
1 cup firmly packed brown sugar
½ cup margarine or butter, softened
½ cup shortening
1 cup peanut butter
1½ teaspoons vanilla
2 eggs
2 cups Pillsbury's BEST® All Purpose or Unbleached Flour
1½ teaspoons baking soda
¼ teaspoon salt
12-oz. pkg. (2 cups) semi-sweet chocolate chips
1 cup chopped salted peanuts

Heat oven to 350°F. In large bowl, beat sugar, brown sugar, margarine and shortening until light and fluffy. Add peanut butter, vanilla and eggs; blend well. Lightly spoon flour into measuring cup; level off. Stir in flour, baking soda, salt, chocolate chips and peanuts; mix well. If necessary, refrigerate about 45 minutes for easier handling.

Shape dough into 1-inch balls; place on ungreased cookie sheets. Flatten with bottom of glass dipped in sugar. Bake at 350°F. for 10 to 13 minutes or until light brown. 7 dozen cookies.

HIGH ALTITUDE—Above 3500 Feet: No change.

NUTRITION INFORMATION PER SERVING

SERVING SIZE: 1 COOKIE		PERCENT U.S. RDA PER SERVING	
CALORIES	100	PROTEIN	2%
PROTEIN	2g	VITAMIN A	*
CARBOHYDRATE	10g	VITAMIN C	*
FAT	6g	THIAMINE	2%
CHOLESTEROL	6mg	RIBOFLAVIN	*
SODIUM	65mg	NIACIN	4%
POTASSIUM	60mg	CALCIUM	*
		IRON	2%

*Contains less than 2% of the U.S. RDA of this nutrient.

Nutmeg adds a special flavor twist to this drop cookie. Its firm texture makes it a good choice for mailing.

Raisin Coconut Cookies

2 cups raisins
1 cup water
1½ cups firmly packed brown sugar
1½ cups margarine or butter, softened
2 teaspoons vanilla
2 eggs
3½ cups Pillsbury's BEST® All Purpose or Unbleached Flour
1½ teaspoons baking soda
1 teaspoon salt
1 teaspoon nutmeg
1 cup coconut
1 cup chopped nuts, if desired

In small saucepan, simmer raisins in water about 5 minutes or until plump. Drain well; cool.

Heat oven to 375°F. Lightly grease cookie sheets. In large bowl, combine brown sugar, margarine, vanilla and eggs; beat well. Lightly spoon flour into measuring cup; level off. Stir in flour, baking soda, salt and nutmeg; mix well. Stir in raisins, coconut and nuts. Drop by rounded teaspoonfuls onto prepared cookie sheets. Bake at 375°F. for 8 to 12 minutes or until edges are light golden brown. 6 dozen cookies.

HIGH ALTITUDE—Above 3500 Feet: No change.

NUTRITION INFORMATION PER SERVING

SERVING SIZE: 1 COOKIE		PERCENT U.S. RDA PER SERVING	
CALORIES	100	PROTEIN	*
PROTEIN	1g	VITAMIN A	2%
CARBOHYDRATE	13g	VITAMIN C	*
FAT	5g	THIAMINE	4%
CHOLESTEROL	8mg	RIBOFLAVIN	*
SODIUM	100mg	NIACIN	*
POTASSIUM	70mg	CALCIUM	2%
		IRON	2%

*Contains less than 2% of the U.S. RDA of this nutrient.

Think of early spring, when the sap starts flowing from the maple trees, and the smell of maple syrup being prepared. Duplicate that smell in your kitchen with this rich, maple-flavored cookie full of toasted pecans.

Northwoods Maple Nut Cookies

6 cups Pillsbury's BEST® All Purpose or Unbleached Flour
1½ teaspoons cream of tartar
1 teaspoon baking powder
1 teaspoon salt
2 cups sugar
1 cup firmly packed brown sugar
1½ cups margarine or butter, softened
1 cup oil
5 teaspoons maple flavor
3 eggs
2 cups toasted, chopped pecans*

Lightly spoon flour into measuring cup; level off. In large bowl, combine flour, cream of tartar, baking powder and salt; set aside. In large bowl, beat sugar, brown sugar, margarine, oil, maple flavor and eggs until well blended. Gradually stir in flour mixture; mix well. Stir in nuts. Cover with plastic wrap; refrigerate at least 1 hour or until firm.

Heat oven to 375°F. Shape dough into 1-inch balls. Place 2 inches apart on ungreased cookie sheets. Flatten with bottom of glass dipped in sugar. Bake at 375°F. for 8 to 10 minutes or until light golden brown. 10 dozen cookies.

TIP: *To toast pecans, spread nuts on cookie sheet; bake at 375°F. for 6 to 10 minutes or until light golden brown.

HIGH ALTITUDE—Above 3500 Feet: No change.

NUTRITION INFORMATION PER SERVING

SERVING SIZE: 1 COOKIE		PERCENT U.S. RDA PER SERVING	
CALORIES	100	PROTEIN	*
PROTEIN	1g	VITAMIN A	2%
CARBOHYDRATE	10g	VITAMIN C	*
FAT	6g	THIAMINE	4%
CHOLESTEROL	6mg	RIBOFLAVIN	*
SODIUM	50mg	NIACIN	*
POTASSIUM	25mg	CALCIUM	*
		IRON	2%

*Contains less than 2% of the U.S. RDA of this nutrient.

A variation of one of our most popular and requested Bake-Off® Contest recipes.

Oatmeal Chocolitas

CRUST
2 cups Pillsbury's BEST® All Purpose or Unbleached Flour
2 cups quick-cooking rolled oats
1½ cups firmly packed brown sugar
1 teaspoon baking soda
½ teaspoon salt
1¼ cups margarine or butter, melted

FILLING
1 cup peanut butter chips
1 cup chocolate or chocolate fudge ice cream topping
3 tablespoons flour

Heat oven to 350°F. Grease 15x10-inch jelly roll pan. Lightly spoon flour into measuring cup; level off. In large bowl, combine all crust ingredients at low speed until crumbly. Press half of crumb mixture, about 2½ cups, in prepared pan. Reserve remaining crumb mixture for topping. Bake at 350°F. for 8 minutes.

Sprinkle warm base with peanut butter chips. In small bowl, combine chocolate topping and flour; pour evenly over chips. Sprinkle with reserved crumbs. Return to oven and bake 16 to 22 minutes or until golden brown. Cool completely. Cut into bars. 48 bars.

HIGH ALTITUDE—Above 3500 Feet: No change.

NUTRITION INFORMATION PER SERVING

SERVING SIZE: 1 BAR		PERCENT U.S. RDA PER SERVING	
CALORIES	140	PROTEIN	2%
PROTEIN	2g	VITAMIN A	4%
CARBOHYDRATE	19g	VITAMIN C	*
FAT	6g	THIAMINE	4%
CHOLESTEROL	0mg	RIBOFLAVIN	*
SODIUM	115mg	NIACIN	2%
POTASSIUM	85mg	CALCIUM	2%
		IRON	4%

*Contains less than 2% of the U.S. RDA of this nutrient.

An eye-appealing and flavorful variation on an extra special favorite.

Honey Roasted Peanut Cookies

COOKIES

1½	cups firmly packed brown sugar
¾	cup sugar
1½	cups margarine or butter, softened
1½	cups peanut butter
½	cup honey
1½	teaspoons vanilla
3	eggs
3¾	cups Pillsbury's BEST® All Purpose or Unbleached Flour
1½	teaspoons baking soda
1	teaspoon salt

GLAZE

⅓	cup creamy peanut butter
3	tablespoons honey
¼	cup hot water
1¼ to 1½	cups powdered sugar
1	cup chopped honey roasted peanuts

Heat oven to 350°F. In large bowl, beat brown sugar, sugar and margarine until light and fluffy. Add peanut butter, honey, vanilla and eggs; blend well. Lightly spoon flour into measuring cup; level off. Stir in flour, baking soda and salt. Drop by rounded teaspoonfuls 2 inches apart onto ungreased cookie sheets. Flatten slightly in crisscross pattern with a fork dipped in flour. Bake at 350°F. for 9 to 12 minutes or until golden brown. Remove from cookie sheets; cool completely.

In medium bowl, combine peanut butter, honey and water; blend well. Stir in enough powdered sugar for desired drizzling consistency. Drizzle over cookies. Sprinkle ½ teaspoon of the chopped nuts over each cookie; allow to set before storing. 8 dozen cookies.

HIGH ALTITUDE—Above 3500 Feet: No change.

NUTRITION INFORMATION PER SERVING

SERVING SIZE: 1 COOKIE		PERCENT U.S. RDA PER SERVING	
CALORIES	110	PROTEIN	4%
PROTEIN	2g	VITAMIN A	2%
CARBOHYDRATE	13g	VITAMIN C	*
FAT	6g	THIAMINE	2%
CHOLESTEROL	8mg	RIBOFLAVIN	*
SODIUM	100mg	NIACIN	6%
POTASSIUM	65mg	CALCIUM	*
		IRON	2%

*Contains less than 2% of the U.S. RDA of this nutrient.

A breeze to make; just press the dough into the baking pan.

Shortbread Pan Cookies

1	egg, separated
¼	teaspoon maple flavor
1	pkg. Pillsbury Plus White Cake Mix
½	cup margarine or butter, softened
3-oz.	pkg. cream cheese, softened
¾	cup chopped pecans

Heat oven to 375°F. In small bowl, beat egg white and maple flavor until stiff; set aside. In large bowl, combine cake mix, margarine, cream cheese and egg yolk at low speed until crumbly. Press in ungreased 15x10-inch jelly roll pan; spread with egg white mixture. Sprinkle with pecans; press lightly. Bake at 375°F. for 15 to 20 minutes or until golden brown. Cool; cut into cookies. 4 dozen cookies.

HIGH ALTITUDE—Above 3500 Feet: No change.

NUTRITION INFORMATION PER SERVING

SERVING SIZE: 1 COOKIE		PERCENT U.S. RDA PER SERVING	
CALORIES	80	PROTEIN	*
PROTEIN	1g	VITAMIN A	2%
CARBOHYDRATE	9g	VITAMIN C	*
FAT	5g	THIAMINE	2%
CHOLESTEROL	8mg	RIBOFLAVIN	*
SODIUM	100mg	NIACIN	*
POTASSIUM	15mg	CALCIUM	*
		IRON	*

*Contains less than 2% of the U.S. RDA of this nutrient.

Supreme Chocolate Mint Chip Cookies pg.34
Honey Roasted Peanut Cookies pg.32

A moist, chewy, frosted, fudge cookie flavored with mint chocolate chips. For a pleasing variation, shape dough into 1½-inch balls, bake and serve without frosting.

Supreme Chocolate Mint Chip Cookies

COOKIES
4	cups Pillsbury's BEST® All Purpose or Unbleached Flour
1	cup unsweetened cocoa
1	teaspoon baking soda
½	teaspoon salt
1½	cups sugar
1	cup firmly packed brown sugar
1½	cups margarine or butter, softened
3	eggs
10-oz.	pkg. (1½ cups) mint chocolate chips

GLAZE
2	cups sugar
½	cup unsweetened cocoa
½	cup margarine or butter
½	cup milk
1	teaspoon vanilla

Heat oven to 350°F. Lightly grease cookie sheets. Lightly spoon flour into measuring cup; level off. In large bowl, combine flour, cocoa, baking soda and salt; set aside. In large bowl, beat sugar, brown sugar and margarine until light and fluffy. Add eggs; blend well. Stir in flour mixture; mix well. Stir in mint chips. Drop by tablespoonfuls 3 inches apart onto prepared cookie sheets; flatten slightly. Bake at 350°F. for 8 to 10 minutes or until set. Cool 1 minute; remove from cookie sheets. Cool completely.

In small saucepan, combine all glaze ingredients except vanilla. Bring to a boil; boil 1 minute. Stir in vanilla; cool.* Beat until smooth and of glaze consistency. Glaze cooled cookies; allow glaze to set. 6 dozen cookies.

TIP: *To cool glaze quickly, place saucepan on ice in large bowl.

HIGH ALTITUDE—Above 3500 Feet: Increase flour to 4 cups plus 2 tablespoons. Bake as directed above.

NUTRITION INFORMATION PER SERVING

SERVING SIZE: 1 COOKIE		PERCENT U.S. RDA PER SERVING	
CALORIES	150	PROTEIN	2%
PROTEIN	2g	VITAMIN A	4%
CARBOHYDRATE	21g	VITAMIN C	*
FAT	7g	THIAMINE	2%
CHOLESTEROL	10mg	RIBOFLAVIN	2%
SODIUM	105mg	NIACIN	2%
POTASSIUM	50mg	CALCIUM	2%
		IRON	4%

*Contains less than 2% of the U.S. RDA of this nutrient.

The lemon peel in this recipe can be grated using your food processor. Remove the outer colored layer of one medium lemon in strips using a vegetable peeler. Process the strips with the ½ cup sugar until finely grated.

Nut-Edged Lemon Cookie Slices

- ½ cup sugar
- ¾ cup firmly packed brown sugar
- 1 cup margarine or butter, softened
- 1½ teaspoons vanilla
- 2 eggs, reserving 1 egg white
- 3 cups Pillsbury's BEST® All Purpose or Unbleached Flour
- 1 tablespoon grated lemon peel
- 1½ teaspoons baking powder
- ¾ teaspoon salt
- ¾ cup finely chopped nuts
- ¼ cup sugar

In large bowl, combine ½ cup sugar, brown sugar, margarine, vanilla, whole egg and egg yolk; beat well. Lightly spoon flour into measuring cup; level off. Stir in flour, lemon peel, baking powder and salt; mix well. Divide dough into thirds on 3 sheets of waxed paper; shape each third into roll 1½ inches in diameter. Wrap; refrigerate until easy to handle, about 1 hour. Combine nuts and ¼ cup sugar. Slightly beat reserved egg white. Brush chilled dough with egg white; roll in nut mixture, pressing nuts firmly into dough. Refrigerate cookies until ready to bake.

Heat oven to 425°F. Lightly grease cookie sheets. Cut dough into ¼-inch slices. Place 1 inch apart on prepared cookie sheets. Bake at 425°F. for 5 to 7 minutes or until light brown. Immediately remove from cookie sheets. 6 to 7 dozen cookies.

🥣 FOOD PROCESSOR DIRECTIONS: Place ¾ cup unchopped nuts and ¼ cup sugar in food processor bowl with metal blade. Cover; process with on/off turns until finely chopped. Remove; set aside. In same food processor bowl, place ½ cup sugar and peel of 1 medium lemon; process until finely grated. Add room-temperature margarine cut into 1-inch pieces, brown sugar, vanilla, whole egg and egg yolk. Cover; process until light and fluffy, stopping to scrape down sides of bowl once or twice. Add flour, baking powder and salt. Cover; process using on/off turns just until flour is incorporated. (Do not over process or cookies will be tough.) Continue as directed above.

TIP: Cookie dough keeps up to 2 weeks in refrigerator and up to 6 weeks in freezer. Slice and bake frozen dough as directed above.

📟 MICROWAVE DIRECTIONS: Prepare cookie dough as directed above. Using inverted 9-inch round or square microwave-safe dish, place 6 dough slices in spoke fashion, spacing evenly apart. Microwave on HIGH for 1¾ to 2 minutes or until no fingerprint remains when lightly touched with finger, rotating dish once halfway through cooking. Immediately remove from dish.

TIP: A microwave-safe baking sheet or microwave-safe pizza dish can be substituted for inverted 9-inch microwave-safe dish.

HIGH ALTITUDE—Above 3500 Feet: No change.

NUTRITION INFORMATION PER SERVING

SERVING SIZE: 1 COOKIE		PERCENT U.S. RDA PER SERVING	
CALORIES	60	PROTEIN	*
PROTEIN	1g	VITAMIN A	*
CARBOHYDRATE	7g	VITAMIN C	*
FAT	3g	THIAMINE	2%
CHOLESTEROL	6mg	RIBOFLAVIN	*
SODIUM	50mg	NIACIN	*
POTASSIUM	20mg	CALCIUM	*
		IRON	*

*Contains less than 2% of the U.S. RDA of this nutrient.

Best-Ever
BARS

Best-Ever
BARS

Sumptuous squares and brag-about bars...

What could be easier than soft, spreadable dough simply baked in a pan with no need to drop, shape, roll or press? The results? Some of America's favorites—brownies, fruit-filled squares and luscious layered creations!

Our recipes feature blue-ribbon flavor combinations—cherry and almond, apples and butterscotch, chocolate and coconut, banana and marshmallow, to name a few. And, there are tasty treats for all occasions—snacking, toting, mailing, casual serving and special desserts. Filled, frosted, layered, glazed or meringue-topped, the choice is yours! Of course, there are some streamlined ideas, too, with mixes or refrigerated doughs to make preparation all the faster.

Before serving, allow bars to cool in the pan. For even squares, "score" top lightly before cutting. Bars can be stored right in the baking pan for added convenience. Just cover tightly and refrigerate if necessary. For toting to potluck or picnic, leave bars in pan until time to serve. They will stay fresher and look better on arrival. When it comes to mailing, bars which are rich, moist and cake-like are good travelers.

A mint-flavored cream cheese filling is swirled through a luscious chocolate brownie.

Gourmet Mint Brownies

BROWNIES

8-oz.	pkg. cream cheese, softened
¼	cup sugar
1	egg
1	teaspoon mint extract
4	drops green food coloring
1	cup margarine or butter
4	oz. (4 squares) unsweetened chocolate, cut into pieces
2	cups sugar
2	teaspoons vanilla
4	eggs
1 to 1¼	cups Pillsbury's BEST® All Purpose or Unbleached Flour

FROSTING

2	tablespoons margarine or butter
2	tablespoons corn syrup
2	tablespoons water
2	oz. (2 squares) unsweetened chocolate, cut into pieces
1	teaspoon vanilla
1	cup powdered sugar

Heat oven to 350°F. Grease and flour 13x9-inch pan. In small bowl, beat cream cheese and ¼ cup sugar until smooth. Add egg, mint extract and food coloring; mix well. Set aside.

In large saucepan, melt 1 cup margarine and 4 oz. chocolate over very low heat, stirring constantly. Remove from heat; cool slightly. Stir in 2 cups sugar and 2 teaspoons vanilla. Add eggs one at a time, beating well after each addition. Lightly spoon flour into measuring cup; level off. Stir in flour; mix well. Spread in prepared pan. Carefully spoon prepared cheese filling over brownie mixture. Gently cut through layers with knife to marble. Bake at 350°F. for 45 to 50 minutes or until set. Cool completely.

In heavy saucepan, bring 2 tablespoons margarine, corn syrup and water to a rolling boil. Remove from heat. Add 2 oz. chocolate; stir until melted. Stir in 1 teaspoon vanilla and enough powdered sugar for desired spreading consistency; beat until smooth. Frost cooled bars. Cut into bars. Store in refrigerator, if desired. 36 bars.

HIGH ALTITUDE—Above 3500 Feet: No change.

NUTRITION INFORMATION PER SERVING

SERVING SIZE: 1 BAR		PERCENT U.S. RDA PER SERVING	
CALORIES	180	PROTEIN	2%
PROTEIN	2g	VITAMIN A	6%
CARBOHYDRATE	20g	VITAMIN C	*
FAT	11g	THIAMINE	2%
CHOLESTEROL	45mg	RIBOFLAVIN	2%
SODIUM	95mg	NIACIN	*
POTASSIUM	65mg	CALCIUM	2%
		IRON	4%

*Contains less than 2% of the U.S. RDA of this nutrient.

Shown on pages 36 and 37 —
Macadamia Wedges pg.40
Gourmet Mint Brownies pg.39

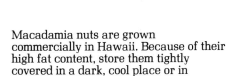

Macadamia nuts are grown commercially in Hawaii. Because of their high fat content, store them tightly covered in a dark, cool place or in the refrigerator.

Macadamia Wedges

1¾ cups Pillsbury's BEST® All Purpose or Unbleached Flour
¾ cup sugar
¼ teaspoon salt
1 cup butter
1 teaspoon vanilla
1 egg yolk
6-oz. pkg. (1 cup) semi-sweet chocolate chips
3½-oz. jar (¾ cup) coarsely chopped macadamia nuts

Heat oven to 325°F. Lightly spoon flour into measuring cup; level off. In large bowl, combine flour, sugar and salt. Using pastry blender or fork, cut in butter until mixture resembles coarse crumbs. Add vanilla and egg yolk; blend until mixture holds together. Divide dough in half. Press each half in ungreased 8-inch round pan. Bake at 325°F. for 35 to 40 minutes or until golden brown. Remove from oven; place on wire rack. Immediately sprinkle ½ cup of the chocolate chips over each baked crust. Let stand until chocolate is melted; spread evenly. Sprinkle nuts evenly over chocolate in each pan, carefully pressing into chocolate. Immediately cut each circle into 12 wedges. Cool completely. 24 wedges.

NUTRITION INFORMATION PER SERVING

SERVING SIZE: 1 WEDGE		PERCENT U.S. RDA PER SERVING	
CALORIES	200	PROTEIN	2%
PROTEIN	2g	VITAMIN A	6%
CARBOHYDRATE	18g	VITAMIN C	*
FAT	14g	THIAMINE	4%
CHOLESTEROL	30mg	RIBOFLAVIN	2%
SODIUM	100mg	NIACIN	2%
POTASSIUM	55mg	CALCIUM	2%
		IRON	4%

*Contains less than 2% of the U.S. RDA of this nutrient.

Short on time, but need a treat to take to a meeting? Try these simple mix-in-the-pan bars.

Choco-Chip Bars

1 pkg. Pillsbury Banana, Date or Nut Quick Bread Mix
1 cup water
1 egg, slightly beaten
6-oz. pkg. (1 cup) semi-sweet chocolate chips
½ cup chopped nuts, if desired

Heat oven to 375°F. Grease and flour bottom only of 13x9-inch pan. Place quick bread mix in pan; add water, egg and ½ cup of the chocolate chips. Stir with fork just until blended, about 2 minutes. (Be sure to blend all dry mix from corners of pan.) Spread batter evenly in pan. Sprinkle remaining chocolate chips and nuts evenly over batter. Bake at 375°F. for 15 to 20 minutes or until toothpick inserted in center comes out clean. Cool; cut into bars. 36 bars.

HIGH ALTITUDE—Above 3500 Feet: Add 1 tablespoon flour to dry quick bread mix. Bake as directed above.

NUTRITION INFORMATION PER SERVING

SERVING SIZE: 1 BAR		PERCENT U.S. RDA PER SERVING	
CALORIES	90	PROTEIN	*
PROTEIN	1g	VITAMIN A	*
CARBOHYDRATE	12g	VITAMIN C	*
FAT	4g	THIAMINE	2%
CHOLESTEROL	8mg	RIBOFLAVIN	2%
SODIUM	50mg	NIACIN	*
POTASSIUM	35mg	CALCIUM	*
		IRON	2%

*Contains less than 2% of the U.S. RDA of this nutrient.

An unbeatable pair: rich chocolate and
moist, chewy coconut!

Chocolate Frosted Toffees

BARS
¾	cup Pillsbury's BEST® All Purpose or Unbleached Flour
⅓	cup firmly packed brown sugar
¼	teaspoon salt
¼	cup margarine or butter, softened
14-oz.	can sweetened condensed milk (not evaporated)
½	cup dark corn syrup
2	teaspoons vanilla
4	cups flaked coconut, toasted*

FROSTING
6-oz.	pkg. (1 cup) semi-sweet chocolate chips
3 to 4	tablespoons whipping cream or milk
½	cup powdered sugar
2	tablespoons margarine or butter, softened
1	teaspoon vanilla

Heat oven to 350°F. Generously grease
13x9-inch pan. Lightly spoon flour into
measuring cup; level off. In large bowl,
combine all bar ingredients except
coconut; mix well. Stir in coconut.
Spread in prepared pan. Bake at 350°F.
for 25 to 35 minutes or until golden
brown. Cool.

In small saucepan over low heat, melt
chocolate chips in whipping cream,
stirring constantly. Stir in powdered
sugar, 2 tablespoons margarine and
1 teaspoon vanilla; mix well. Spread
over bars. Refrigerate 30 minutes; cut
into bars. 48 bars.

TIP: *To toast coconut, spread on cookie
sheet; bake at 350°F. for 12 to
16 minutes or until golden brown.

HIGH ALTITUDE—Above 3500 Feet:
No change.

NUTRITION INFORMATION PER SERVING

SERVING SIZE: 1 BAR		PERCENT U.S. RDA PER SERVING	
CALORIES	130	PROTEIN	2%
PROTEIN	1g	VITAMIN A	2%
CARBOHYDRATE	17g	VITAMIN C	*
FAT	6g	THIAMINE	*
CHOLESTEROL	4mg	RIBOFLAVIN	2%
SODIUM	45mg	NIACIN	*
POTASSIUM	85mg	CALCIUM	4%
		IRON	2%

*Contains less than 2% of the U.S. RDA of this nutrient.

For the sweet tooth partial to caramel and chocolate, this is the bar that will please. A caution when melting chocolate: excessive heat or water drops in melted chocolate can cause it to stiffen. Should this happen, stir melted shortening into the stiffened chocolate (1½ teaspoons shortening for each ½ cup chips).

Krispy Chocolate Caramel Bars

CRUST
- 1¼ cups Pillsbury's BEST® All Purpose or Unbleached Flour
- ½ cup powdered sugar
- ½ cup margarine or butter

FILLING
- 14-oz. pkg. vanilla caramels
- ⅓ cup half-and-half or evaporated milk
- ¼ cup margarine or butter

TOPPING
- 6-oz. pkg. (1 cup) semi-sweet chocolate chips
- 3 tablespoons shortening
- ¾ cup crisp rice cereal

Heat oven to 350°F. Lightly spoon flour into measuring cup; level off. In medium bowl, combine flour and powdered sugar Using pastry blender or fork, cut in ½ cup margarine until crumbly. Lightly press mixture in ungreased 13x9-inch pan. Bake at 350°F. for 10 to 12 minutes or until light brown.

Meanwhile, in heavy saucepan melt caramels, half-and-half and ¼ cup margarine over low heat, stirring constantly. Spread over baked crust.

In medium saucepan over low heat, melt chocolate chips and shortening, stirring constantly. Stir in cereal. Carefully spread over filling. Cool completely; cut into bars. 36 bars.

■ MICROWAVE DIRECTIONS: Prepare crust as directed above. In 4-cup microwave-safe measuring cup, combine caramels, half-and-half and ¼ cup margarine. Microwave on HIGH for 3 to 4 minutes or until mixture is smooth, stirring twice during cooking. Spread over baked crust.

In 2-cup microwave-safe measuring cup, combine chocolate chips with shortening Microwave on HIGH for 1¼ to 1½ minutes or until melted, stirring once halfway through cooking. Stir until smooth. Stir in cereal. Carefully spread over filling.

NUTRITION INFORMATION PER SERVING

SERVING SIZE: 1 BAR		PERCENT U.S. RDA PER SERVING	
CALORIES	140	PROTEIN	2%
PROTEIN	1g	VITAMIN A	4%
CARBOHYDRATE	17g	VITAMIN C	*
FAT	8g	THIAMINE	2%
CHOLESTEROL	0mg	RIBOFLAVIN	2%
SODIUM	80mg	NIACIN	*
POTASSIUM	50mg	CALCIUM	2%
		IRON	2%

*Contains less than 2% of the U.S. RDA of this nutrient.

Krispy Chocolate Caramel Bar

Banana lovers will delight in this easy bar!

Double Banana Marshmallow Squares

BASE
- 1 pkg. Pillsbury Plus Banana or Yellow Cake Mix
- 1 cup rolled oats
- ⅓ cup margarine or butter, softened
- 1 egg

FILLING
- 1 cup mashed bananas
- 4 cups miniature marshmallows
- 3½-oz. pkg. instant vanilla pudding and pie filling mix

Heat oven to 350°F. Grease and flour 13x9-inch pan. In large bowl, combine all base ingredients; mix at low speed until crumbly. Reserve ½ cup crumb mixture for topping. Press remaining crumbs firmly in bottom of prepared pan.

In large saucepan, heat all filling ingredients over low heat until marshmallows melt, stirring constantly. Spread filling evenly over crust. Sprinkle reserved crumb mixture over filling.

Bake at 350°F. for 25 to 30 minutes or until light golden brown. Cool completely; cut into bars. 36 bars.

HIGH ALTITUDE—Above 3500 Feet: Bake at 375°F. for 30 to 40 minutes.

NUTRITION INFORMATION PER SERVING

SERVING SIZE: 1 BAR		PERCENT U.S. RDA PER SERVING	
CALORIES	120	PROTEIN	2%
PROTEIN	1g	VITAMIN A	*
CARBOHYDRATE	21g	VITAMIN C	*
FAT	3g	THIAMINE	4%
CHOLESTEROL	8mg	RIBOFLAVIN	2%
SODIUM	125mg	NIACIN	*
POTASSIUM	45mg	CALCIUM	2%
		IRON	2%

*Contains less than 2% of the U.S. RDA of this nutrient.

Surprised by unexpected guests? Treat them with this sure-to-please, microwave sweet.

Crescent Chocolate Almond Toffee

- ¾ cup graham cracker crumbs
- 8-oz. can Pillsbury Refrigerated Quick Crescent Dinner Rolls
- 1 cup firmly packed brown sugar
- 1 cup margarine or butter
- ¾ cup sliced almonds
- 1 to 1½ cups semi-sweet chocolate chips

■ MICROWAVE DIRECTIONS: Lightly grease 12x12-inch microwave-safe pan or 13x9-inch microwave-safe baking dish; sprinkle with 2 teaspoons of the graham cracker crumbs. Unroll dough into 2 long rectangles. Place in prepared pan; press over bottom to form crust. Seal perforations. Microwave on HIGH for 4½ to 5½ minutes or until no longer doughy, rotating pan every 1½ minutes. Sprinkle cooked crust with remaining graham cracker crumbs.

In 1½-quart microwave-safe bowl, microwave brown sugar and margarine on HIGH for 2 minutes; stir until smooth. Microwave on high an additional 1½ to 2½ minutes; stir again until smooth. Drizzle over cooked crust; sprinkle with almonds. Microwave on HIGH for 4 to 5 minutes or until brown sugar mixture bubbly over entire surface, rotating pan every 1½ minutes. Cool on flat surface for 2 minutes; sprinkle with chocolate chips. Let chocolate chips soften; carefully marble over top of bars. Let chocolate set before cutting into bars. Remove from pan before storing. Refrigerate, if desired. 36 to 48 bars.

NUTRITION INFORMATION PER SERVING

SERVING SIZE: 1 BAR		PERCENT U.S. RDA PER SERVING	
CALORIES	110	PROTEIN	*
PROTEIN	1g	VITAMIN A	2%
CARBOHYDRATE	11g	VITAMIN C	*
FAT	7g	THIAMINE	*
CHOLESTEROL	0mg	RIBOFLAVIN	2%
SODIUM	95mg	NIACIN	*
POTASSIUM	60mg	CALCIUM	*
		IRON	2%

*Contains less than 2% of the U.S. RDA of this nutrient.

Creamy fudge over a chewy graham cracker layer combines for a rich, candy-like, no-bake bar.

Double Layer Fudge Bars

BASE
1 cup sugar
¼ cup unsweetened cocoa
⅔ cup margarine or butter
2 eggs
1 teaspoon vanilla
32 squares graham crackers, coarsely crushed (3½ cups)
½ cup sunflower nuts
½ cup coconut

TOPPING
2 cups sugar
¾ cup evaporated milk
6-oz. pkg. (1 cup) semi-sweet chocolate chips
7-oz. jar marshmallow creme
½ cup margarine or butter

In saucepan over low heat, combine 1 cup sugar, cocoa, ⅔ cup margarine and eggs. Heat until mixture is bubbly, about 7 minutes, stirring occasionally. Remove from heat; stir in vanilla, graham cracker crumbs, sunflower nuts and coconut. Spread evenly in ungreased 13x9-inch pan. Press down gently; cool.

In large heavy saucepan over medium heat, combine 2 cups sugar and evaporated milk; blend well. Cook until candy thermometer reaches soft ball stage (234°F.). Add chocolate chips, marshmallow creme and ½ cup margarine; stir until ingredients are melted and well combined. Pour mixture on cooled base. Cool completely; cut into bars. Store at room temperature. 48 bars.

Cranberries don't need to be in season to make this wonderful, frosted, cake-like bar; just use the Cranberry Quick Bread Mix from your shelf.

Cranberry Sour Cream Bars

BARS
1 pkg. Pillsbury Cranberry Quick Bread Mix
8-oz. carton dairy sour cream
⅓ cup water
½ teaspoon almond extract
1 egg

FROSTING
1¼ cups powdered sugar
⅓ cup margarine or butter, softened
1 tablespoon lemon juice
¼ cup sliced almonds

Heat oven to 375°F. Grease bottom of 13x9-inch pan. In large bowl, combine all bar ingredients; stir 50 to 75 strokes by hand until dry particles are moistened. Spread in prepared pan. Bake at 375°F. for 20 to 25 minutes or until toothpick inserted in center comes out clean. Cool completely.

In small bowl, blend all frosting ingredients except almonds until smooth. Frost cooled bars. Sprinkle with sliced almonds. Cut into bars. 36 bars.

HIGH ALTITUDE—Above 3500 Feet: Add 2 tablespoons flour to dry quick bread mix. Bake as directed above.

Subtle lemon and chocolate in a fun bar that will please kids of all ages.

Lemon Marshmallow Bars

CRUST
1 ½ cups Pillsbury's BEST® All
     Purpose or Unbleached
     Flour
  ¾ cup powdered sugar
  ¾ cup margarine or butter
FILLING
  ½ cup water
   2 envelopes unflavored gelatin
   2 cups sugar
  ½ cup water
   1 teaspoon lemon extract
8-12 drops yellow food coloring
   1 tablespoon grated lemon peel
GLAZE
   1 cup milk chocolate chips
   3 tablespoons shortening

Heat oven to 350ºF. Lightly spoon flour into measuring cup; level off. In medium bowl, combine flour and powdered sugar. Using pastry blender or fork, cut in margarine until crumbly. Press mixture in ungreased 13x9-inch pan. Bake at 350ºF. for 15 to 18 minutes or until light golden brown. Cool.

Meanwhile, in large bowl combine ½ cup water and gelatin; set aside. In medium saucepan, combine sugar and ½ cup water; bring to a boil. Boil 2 minutes. Pour over gelatin; mix well. Cool 5 minutes in refrigerator. Beat 8 to 10 minutes at **highest** speed or until very thick. Add lemon extract and food coloring; beat well. Fold in lemon peel. Pour over cooled crust. Refrigerate to set.

In small saucepan over low heat, melt milk chocolate chips with shortening, stirring constantly. Spread or drizzle over filling. Cut into bars; cool completely. 36 bars.

Lemon Marshmallow Bars

The appealing flavors of rum and raspberry blend together in this melt-in-your-mouth, meringue-topped bar.

Rum Raspberry Meringue Squares

CRUST
  ½ cup sugar
  ½ cup margarine or butter,
     softened
   2 egg yolks
   1 cup Pillsbury's BEST® All
     Purpose or Unbleached Flour
  ¼ teaspoon baking soda
  ¼ teaspoon salt
FILLING
  ½ cup raspberry jam
  ½ teaspoon rum extract
MERINGUE
   2 egg whites
  ¼ cup sugar
   2 tablespoons finely chopped
     walnuts, if desired

Heat oven to 350ºF. Grease bottom only of 9-inch square pan. In small bowl, beat ½ cup sugar and margarine until light and fluffy. Add egg yolks; blend well. Lightly spoon flour into measuring cup; level off. Stir in flour, baking soda and salt; mix well. Press in bottom of prepared pan. Bake at 350ºF. for 15 minutes.

In small bowl, combine jam and rum extract; spread over crust. In small bowl, beat egg whites until soft peaks form. Gradually add ¼ cup sugar, beating until stiff peaks form. Carefully spread meringue over jam layer. Sprinkle with chopped walnuts. Return to oven and bake an additional 13 to 18 minutes or until meringue is light golden brown. While warm, cut into squares. 25 squares.

TIP: For easier cutting of squares, dip knife in hot water.

HIGH ALTITUDE—Above 3500 Feet: No change.

In this sweet treat, an irresistible combination of applesauce and butterscotch is sandwiched between a quickly prepared crumb mixture. Serve warm or at room temperature.

Applesauce Crumb Squares

BARS
- 1 pkg. Pillsbury Plus Yellow Cake Mix
- ½ cup margarine or butter, softened
- 1 teaspoon cinnamon
- 1 cup applesauce
- ½ cup butterscotch chips
- ¼ cup chopped nuts
- ¼ cup wheat germ

GLAZE
- 1 cup powdered sugar
- ½ teaspoon vanilla
- 1 to 2 tablespoons milk

Heat oven to 350°F. In large bowl, combine cake mix, margarine and cinnamon at low speed until crumbly. Reserve 1 cup crumb mixture. Press remaining crumbs in ungreased 13x9-inch pan. Bake at 350°F. for 12 minutes. Spread applesauce over crust; sprinkle with butterscotch chips. In small bowl, combine reserved crumb mixture, nuts and wheat germ; mix well. Sprinkle over filling. Bake an additional 15 to 25 minutes or until golden brown.

In small bowl, combine powdered sugar, vanilla and enough milk for desired drizzling consistency. Drizzle glaze over bars. Cut into bars. 36 bars.

HIGH ALTITUDE—Above 3500 Feet: No change.

NUTRITION INFORMATION PER SERVING

SERVING SIZE: 1 BAR		PERCENT U.S. RDA PER SERVING	
CALORIES	120	PROTEIN	*
PROTEIN	1g	VITAMIN A	2%
CARBOHYDRATE	17g	VITAMIN C	*
FAT	5g	THIAMINE	4%
CHOLESTEROL	0mg	RIBOFLAVIN	2%
SODIUM	125mg	NIACIN	*
POTASSIUM	20mg	CALCIUM	*
		IRON	2%

*Contains less than 2% of the U.S. RDA of this nutrient.

Front: Peach Almond Crescent Bars pg.50
Back: Applesauce Crumb Squares pg.48

Flaky crescent rolls form the pastry for this bar, which is filled with a special peach filling.

Peach Almond Crescent Bars

8-oz. can Pillsbury Refrigerated Quick Crescent Dinner Rolls
½ cup peach preserves
½ to 1½ teaspoons grated lemon peel
½ teaspoon almond extract

TOPPING
¼ cup sliced or slivered almonds
2 tablespoons rolled oats
2 tablespoons margarine or butter, melted
2 tablespoons honey

Heat oven to 375°F. Separate dough into 4 rectangles. Place 2 rectangles in ungreased 8 or 9-inch square pan. Press over bottom and ½ inch up sides to form crust. Seal perforations. In small bowl, combine peach preserves, lemon peel and almond extract; spread over crust. Separate 2 remaining rectangles into 4 triangles; place over filling. Combine topping ingredients; gently spread over triangles. Bake at 375°F. for 18 to 23 minutes or until golden brown. Cool 10 minutes. Cut into bars. 20 bars.

NUTRITION INFORMATION PER SERVING

SERVING SIZE: 1 BAR		PERCENT U.S. RDA PER SERVING	
CALORIES	90	PROTEIN	*
PROTEIN	1g	VITAMIN A	*
CARBOHYDRATE	12g	VITAMIN C	*
FAT	4g	THIAMINE	2%
CHOLESTEROL	0mg	RIBOFLAVIN	2%
SODIUM	105mg	NIACIN	*
POTASSIUM	45mg	CALCIUM	*
		IRON	2%

*Contains less than 2% of the U.S. RDA of this nutrient.

A simple brownie mix becomes an epicurean delight.

Frosted Orange Cappuccino Brownies

BROWNIES
½ cup very hot water
1 to 2 tablespoons instant coffee granules or crystals
21½-oz. pkg. Pillsbury Family Size Deluxe Fudge Brownie Mix
½ cup oil
1 tablespoon brandy*
1 tablespoon grated orange peel
1 egg

FROSTING
1 can Pillsbury Frosting Supreme Ready To Spread Chocolate Fudge Frosting

GLAZE
¼ cup powdered sugar
½ teaspoon grated orange peel
1 to 2 teaspoons hot water

Heat oven to 350°F. Grease bottom only of 13x9-inch pan. In large bowl, dissolve instant coffee in hot water. Add remaining brownie ingredients; beat 50 strokes with spoon. Spread in prepared pan. Bake at 350°F. for 30 to 35 minutes or until set. DO NOT OVERBAKE. Cool completely.

Frost cooled brownies with fudge frosting. In small bowl, combine powdered sugar, orange peel and enough water for glaze consistency. Drizzle over frosting. Cut into bars. 36 bars.

TIP: *One teaspoon brandy extract plus 2 teaspoons water can be substituted for brandy.

HIGH ALTITUDE—Above 3500 Feet: Add 2 tablespoons flour to dry brownie mix. Bake as directed above.

NUTRITION INFORMATION PER SERVING

SERVING SIZE: 1 BAR		PERCENT U.S. RDA PER SERVING	
CALORIES	150	PROTEIN	*
PROTEIN	1g	VITAMIN A	*
CARBOHYDRATE	22g	VITAMIN C	*
FAT	7g	THIAMINE	2%
CHOLESTEROL	8mg	RIBOFLAVIN	*
SODIUM	90mg	NIACIN	*
POTASSIUM	45mg	CALCIUM	*
		IRON	*

*Contains less than 2% of the U.S. RDA of this nutrient.

These bars will give you a taste of the tropics.

Hawaiian Pineapple Bars

20-oz. roll Pillsbury's BEST®
Refrigerated Sugar Cookies
8-oz. pkg. cream cheese, softened
½ cup sugar
1 tablespoon lemon juice
1 teaspoon grated lemon peel
½ cup pineapple ice cream
topping
¼ cup shredded coconut
2 tablespoons chopped pecans

Heat oven to 350°F. Spread cookie dough evenly in bottom of ungreased 13x9-inch pan. Bake at 350°F. for 14 to 19 minutes or until golden brown. Cool.

In small bowl, combine cream cheese, sugar, lemon juice and lemon peel; beat until smooth. Spread over cooled cookie base. Spoon pineapple topping on cheese mixture; gently spread. Sprinkle coconut and pecans over topping. Refrigerate at least 1 hour before serving. Cut into bars. 24 to 36 bars.

NUTRITION INFORMATION PER SERVING

SERVING SIZE: 1 BAR		PERCENT U.S. RDA PER SERVING	
CALORIES	110	PROTEIN	*
PROTEIN	1g	VITAMIN A	*
CARBOHYDRATE	15g	VITAMIN C	*
FAT	5g	THIAMINE	2%
CHOLESTEROL	6mg	RIBOFLAVIN	2%
SODIUM	90mg	NIACIN	*
POTASSIUM	20mg	CALCIUM	*
		IRON	2%

*Contains less than 2% of the U.S. RDA of this nutrient.

A coconutty cheesecake layer is sandwiched between German chocolate crumb layers—heavenly!

German Chocolate Dessert Bars

BASE
1 pkg. Pillsbury Plus German
Chocolate Cake Mix
1½ cups quick-cooking rolled oats
½ cup margarine or butter,
softened
1 egg
FILLING
1 can Pillsbury Ready To Spread
Coconut Pecan or Coconut
Almond Frosting Supreme
8-oz. pkg. cream cheese, softened
2 eggs

Heat oven to 350°F. Grease 13x9-inch pan. In large bowl, combine all base ingredients; mix at low speed until crumbly. Reserve 2 cups crumb mixture for topping; press remaining crumb mixture in bottom of prepared pan. In same large bowl, blend all filling ingredients; beat at **highest** speed for one minute. Pour over crust. Sprinkle reserved crumbs over filling.

Bake at 350°F. for 45 to 55 minutes or until toothpick inserted in center comes out clean. Serve warm or cool. Cut into bars. Store in refrigerator. 36 bars.

HIGH ALTITUDE—Above 3500 Feet: Bake at 375°F. for 45 to 55 minutes.

NUTRITION INFORMATION PER SERVING

SERVING SIZE: 1 BAR		PERCENT U.S. RDA PER SERVING	
CALORIES	170	PROTEIN	2%
PROTEIN	2g	VITAMIN A	4%
CARBOHYDRATE	19g	VITAMIN C	*
FAT	10g	THIAMINE	4%
CHOLESTEROL	30mg	RIBOFLAVIN	2%
SODIUM	180mg	NIACIN	*
POTASSIUM	60mg	CALCIUM	2%
		IRON	4%

*Contains less than 2% of the U.S. RDA of this nutrient.

Pine nuts or pignoli is the culinary name for pine cone kernels. They have a mild, unique flavor that is definitely not "piney." Store them lightly covered in a cool, dark place or in the refrigerator.

Pine Nut Cremes

CRUST
- 1 cup Pillsbury's BEST® All Purpose or Unbleached Flour
- 1 cup quick-cooking rolled oats
- ½ cup powdered sugar
- ½ teaspoon baking powder
- ½ cup margarine or butter

FILLING
- ½ cup sugar
- 1 tablespoon flour
- ⅓ cup whipping cream
- ⅓ cup margarine or butter
- 1 cup pine nuts (pignoli), toasted*

Heat oven to 350°F. Lightly grease 13x9-inch pan. Lightly spoon flour into measuring cup; level off. In large bowl, combine 1 cup flour, oats, powdered sugar and baking powder. Using pastry blender or fork, cut in ½ cup margarine until crumbly. Press in prepared pan. Bake at 350°F. for 12 to 15 minutes or until set.

Meanwhile, in small saucepan over medium heat combine sugar, 1 tablespoon flour, whipping cream and ⅓ cup margarine. Bring to full boil; boil 2 minutes, stirring constantly. Pour over crust; sprinkle with pine nuts. Return to oven; bake 5 to 7 minutes longer or until topping bubbles. Cool completely; cut into bars. 36 bars.

TIP: *To toast pine nuts, spread evenly on cookie sheet; bake at 350°F. for 5 to 10 minutes, stirring occasionally.

HIGH ALTITUDE—Above 3500 Feet: No change.

NUTRITION INFORMATION PER SERVING

SERVING SIZE: 1 BAR		PERCENT U.S. RDA PER SERVING	
CALORIES	100	PROTEIN	2%
PROTEIN	2g	VITAMIN A	4%
CARBOHYDRATE	9g	VITAMIN C	*
FAT	7g	THIAMINE	4%
CHOLESTEROL	2mg	RIBOFLAVIN	*
SODIUM	55mg	NIACIN	*
POTASSIUM	35mg	CALCIUM	*
		IRON	2%

*Contains less than 2% of the U.S. RDA of this nutrient.

Pack these great honey-sweetened bars as a snack for your favorite outing.

Oats 'N Honey Bars

- 1 cup margarine or butter, softened
- ⅓ cup honey
- 1 teaspoon vanilla
- 1½ cups Pillsbury's BEST® All Purpose or Unbleached Flour
- 1½ cups quick-cooking rolled oats
- ½ teaspoon salt
- 6-oz. pkg. (1 cup) butterscotch chips

Heat oven to 350°F. In large bowl, combine margarine, honey and vanilla; beat until smooth and creamy. Lightly spoon flour into measuring cup; level off. Add flour, oats and salt; mix well. Stir in chips. Press in bottom of ungreased 13x9-inch pan. Bake at 350°F. for 20 to 30 minutes or until light golden brown. 36 bars.

HIGH ALTITUDE—Above 3500 Feet: No change.

NUTRITION INFORMATION PER SERVING

SERVING SIZE: 1 BAR		PERCENT U.S. RDA PER SERVING	
CALORIES	110	PROTEIN	*
PROTEIN	1g	VITAMIN A	4%
CARBOHYDRATE	11g	VITAMIN C	*
FAT	7g	THIAMINE	2%
CHOLESTEROL	0mg	RIBOFLAVIN	*
SODIUM	90mg	NIACIN	*
POTASSIUM	20mg	CALCIUM	*
		IRON	*

*Contains less than 2% of the U.S. RDA of this nutrient.

frosted, cake-type bar with natural sweetness and easy preparation.

Apricot Quick Bars

BARS
- 1½ cups water
- 6-oz. pkg. dried apricots, chopped
- 1 pkg. Pillsbury Nut Quick Bread Mix
- 2 tablespoons oil
- 1 egg

GLAZE
- 2 cups powdered sugar
- 2 tablespoons margarine or butter, softened
- 1 tablespoon lemon juice
- 2 to 3 tablespoons water

In large saucepan, bring water and apricots just to a boil; remove from heat. Cover; let stand 10 minutes or until fruit is tender.

Heat oven to 375°F. Grease and flour 13x9-inch pan. Add quick bread mix, oil and egg to apricot mixture; stir 50 to 75 strokes by hand until dry particles are moistened. Spread in prepared pan. Bake at 375°F. for 20 to 25 minutes or until toothpick inserted in center comes out clean.

In small bowl, blend all glaze ingredients, adding enough water for desired glaze consistency. Drizzle glaze over bars. Cool completely; cut into bars. 36 bars.

HIGH ALTITUDE—Above 3500 Feet: Decrease water to 1¼ cups. Add 1 tablespoon flour to dry quick bread mix. Bake as directed above.

NUTRITION INFORMATION PER SERVING

SERVING SIZE: 1 BAR		PERCENT U.S. RDA PER SERVING	
CALORIES	100	PROTEIN	*
PROTEIN	1g	VITAMIN A	8%
CARBOHYDRATE	19g	VITAMIN C	*
DIETARY FIBER	1g	THIAMINE	12%
FAT	3g	RIBOFLAVIN	12%
POLYUNSATURATED	1g	NIACIN	12%
SATURATED	0g	CALCIUM	*
CHOLESTEROL	6mg	IRON	2%
SODIUM	70mg	*Less than 2% U.S. RDA	
POTASSIUM	80mg		

An ever popular recipe from the first Bake-Off® Contest in 1949.

Hoosier Bars

BARS
- ½ cup sugar
- ½ cup firmly packed brown sugar
- ½ cup margarine or butter, softened
- 1 teaspoon vanilla
- 2 egg yolks
- 1½ cups Pillsbury's BEST® All Purpose or Unbleached Flour
- 1 teaspoon baking soda
- ½ teaspoon salt
- 6-oz. pkg. (1 cup) semi-sweet chocolate chips
- ½ cup chopped salted peanuts

MERINGUE
- 2 egg whites
- 1 cup firmly packed brown sugar
- ¼ cup chopped salted peanuts

Heat oven to 325°F. Grease 13x9-inch pan. In large bowl, beat sugar, ½ cup brown sugar and margarine until light and fluffy. Add vanilla and egg yolks; blend well. Lightly spoon flour into measuring cup; level off. Stir in flour, baking soda and salt; mix well. Press in bottom of prepared pan. Sprinkle chocolate chips and ½ cup peanuts over dough; pat in gently. Set aside.

In small bowl, beat egg whites until soft peaks form; gradually add 1 cup brown sugar, beating until stiff peaks form. Spread over dough mixture. Sprinkle ¼ cup peanuts over meringue; gently press into meringue. Bake at 325°F. for 40 to 45 minutes or until golden brown. While warm, cut into bars. 36 bars.

TIP: For easier cutting of bars, dip knife in hot water.

HIGH ALTITUDE—Above 3500 Feet: No change.

NUTRITION INFORMATION PER SERVING

SERVING SIZE: 1 BAR		PERCENT U.S. RDA PER SERVING	
CALORIES	130	PROTEIN	2%
PROTEIN	2g	VITAMIN A	2%
CARBOHYDRATE	18g	VITAMIN C	*
FAT	6g	THIAMINE	2%
CHOLESTEROL	15mg	RIBOFLAVIN	*
SODIUM	110mg	NIACIN	2%
POTASSIUM	80mg	CALCIUM	2%
		IRON	4%

*Contains less than 2% of the U.S. RDA of this nutrient.

This special occasion bar has a rich, divine flavor and an elegant appearance. It can be cut smaller like a confection.

Raspberry Chocolate Supremes

CRUST
- 1 cup Pillsbury's BEST® All Purpose or Unbleached Flour
- ¼ cup powdered sugar
- ½ cup margarine or butter

FILLING
- ½ cup raspberry jam
- 3-oz. pkg. cream cheese, softened
- 2 tablespoons milk
- 1 cup vanilla milk chips, or 4 oz. white chocolate, melted

GLAZE
- 2 oz. (2 squares) semi-sweet chocolate, cut into pieces
- 1 tablespoon shortening

Heat oven to 375°F. Lightly spoon flour into measuring cup; level off. In medium bowl, combine flour and powdered sugar. Using pastry blender or fork, cut in margarine until crumbly. Press mixture in ungreased 9-inch square pan. Bake at 375°F. for 15 to 17 minutes or until lightly browned.

Spread jam evenly over baked crust. In small bowl, beat cream cheese and milk until smooth. Add melted vanilla chips to cream cheese mixture; beat until smooth. Drop cream cheese mixture by teaspoonfuls evenly over jam; carefully spread to cover. Refrigerate until set.

In small saucepan over low heat, melt chocolate with shortening, stirring constantly. Spread over white chocolate layer. Cool completely; cut into bars. Store in refrigerator. 25 bars.

NUTRITION INFORMATION PER SERVING

SERVING SIZE: 1 BAR		PERCENT U.S. RDA PER SERVING	
CALORIES	140	PROTEIN	*
PROTEIN	1g	VITAMIN A	4%
CARBOHYDRATE	14g	VITAMIN C	*
FAT	9g	THIAMINE	2%
CHOLESTEROL	4mg	RIBOFLAVIN	*
SODIUM	55mg	NIACIN	*
POTASSIUM	50mg	CALCIUM	*
		IRON	2%

*Contains less than 2% of the U.S. RDA of this nutrient.

Front: Raspberry Chocolate Supremes pg.54
Back: Cherry Almond Delights pg.56

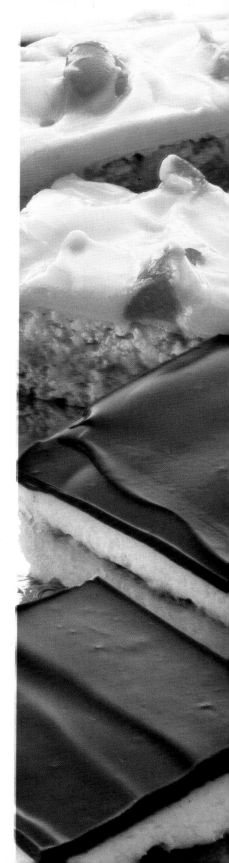

This luscious bar of almond meringue filling on a pastry crust, topped with a cherry buttercream frosting, is perfect for festive occasions. Included in the recipe are food processor directions for making your own almond paste to use in the filling.

Cherry Almond Delights

CRUST
- ½ cup firmly packed brown sugar
- ½ cup margarine or butter, softened
- 1 egg
- 1 ¼ cups Pillsbury's BEST® All Purpose or Unbleached Flour
- ¼ teaspoon salt

FILLING
- 1 cup almond paste or canned almond filling
- ¾ cup sugar
- 1 tablespoon lemon juice
- 2 egg yolks
- 2 egg whites, beaten stiff

FROSTING
- 2 tablespoons margarine or butter, softened
- 1 ½ cups powdered sugar
- 3 to 4 tablespoons cherry juice
- ⅓ cup quartered maraschino cherries, well drained

Heat oven to 350ºF. Grease and flour 13x9-inch pan. In small bowl, beat brown sugar and ½ cup margarine until light and fluffy. Add egg; blend well. Lightly spoon flour into measuring cup; level off. Stir in flour and salt. Spread dough evenly in bottom of prepared pan. Bake at 350ºF. for 11 to 13 minutes or until lightly browned.

In large bowl, combine almond paste, sugar, lemon juice and egg yolks; mix until smooth. Fold in beaten egg whites. Spread over baked crust. Bake at 350ºF. for 20 to 25 minutes or until golden brown and filling is set. Cool.

In small bowl, combine margarine and powdered sugar. Beat in enough cherry juice until light and fluffy and of desired spreading consistency. Fold in cherries. Spread over cooled bars. Cut into bars. 36 bars.

HIGH ALTITUDE—Above 3500 Feet: No change.

🍴 FOOD PROCESSOR DIRECTIONS: To prepare crust, cut room-temperature margarine into 1-inch pieces; place in food processor bowl with metal blade. Add brown sugar and egg. Cover; process until light and fluffy. Lightly spoon flour into measuring cup; level off. Add flour and salt. Cover; process using on/off turns just until flour is incorporated. (Do not over process or crust will be tough.) Spread dough evenly in bottom of prepared pan. Bake as directed above.

To prepare filling, in same food processor bowl combine **1 cup blanched almonds** and ¾ **cup powdered sugar**. Cover; process to a fine powder, about 2 minutes. Scrape down sides of bowl. Add **2 tablespoons water** and ¼ **teaspoon almond extract**. Cover; process 30 seconds or until mixture forms a ball. Add ¾ cup sugar, 1 tablespoon lemon juice and 2 egg yolks. Cover; process just until smooth. Transfer to a large bowl; fold in beaten egg whites. Spread over baked crust. Continue as directed above.

NUTRITION INFORMATION PER SERVING

SERVING SIZE: 1 BAR		PERCENT U.S. RDA PER SERVING	
CALORIES	120	PROTEIN	2%
PROTEIN	2g	VITAMIN A	2%
CARBOHYDRATE	18g	VITAMIN C	*
FAT	5g	THIAMINE	2%
CHOLESTEROL	25mg	RIBOFLAVIN	4%
SODIUM	60mg	NIACIN	2%
POTASSIUM	65mg	CALCIUM	2%
		IRON	2%

*Contains less than 2% of the U.S. RDA of this nutrient.

A delectable, no-bake confectionary with microwave directions.

3-Layer Bars

CRUST
- ½ cup margarine or butter
- ¼ cup unsweetened cocoa
- 2 teaspoons vanilla
- 1 egg, slightly beaten
- 2 cups graham cracker crumbs
- ½ cup powdered sugar
- ½ cup shredded coconut
- ½ cup chopped nuts

FILLING
- ½ cup margarine or butter
- ½ cup milk
- 3⅛-oz. pkg. vanilla pudding and pie filling mix (not instant)
- 3 cups powdered sugar

TOPPING
- 8-oz. bar milk chocolate, cut into pieces
- 1 tablespoon graham cracker crumbs

Grease 13x9-inch pan. In medium saucepan over low heat, melt ½ cup margarine and cocoa. Remove from heat. Add vanilla and egg; mix well. Stir in 2 cups graham cracker crumbs, ½ cup powdered sugar, coconut and nuts; mix well. Press mixture in bottom of prepared pan. Refrigerate.

In medium saucepan over low heat, melt ½ cup margarine. Blend in milk and pudding mix; cook until mixture thickens slightly, about 5 minutes, stirring constantly. Remove from heat. Beat in powdered sugar until smooth. Spread over crust. Refrigerate 20 to 30 minutes or until set.

In small saucepan over low heat, melt chocolate, stirring constantly. Spread evenly over filling. Sprinkle with 1 tablespoon graham cracker crumbs. Refrigerate 10 to 15 minutes to set chocolate; cut into bars. Store in refrigerator. 36 bars.

■ MICROWAVE DIRECTIONS: Grease 13x9-inch pan. In 8-cup microwave-safe measuring cup or 1½-quart round microwave-safe dish, microwave ½ cup margarine and cocoa on HIGH for 45 to 60 seconds or until margarine is melted. Add vanilla and egg; mix well. Stir in 2 cups graham cracker crumbs, ½ cup powdered sugar, coconut and nuts; mix well. Press mixture in bottom of prepared pan. Refrigerate.

Cut ½ cup margarine in 6 pieces. In 8-cup microwave-safe measuring cup or 1½-quart round microwave-safe dish, combine margarine, milk and pudding mix. Microwave on HIGH for 2½ to 3 minutes or until slightly thickened, stirring twice during cooking. Beat in powdered sugar until smooth. Spread over crust. Refrigerate 20 to 30 minutes or until set.

In 2-cup microwave-safe measuring cup, microwave chocolate on MEDIUM for 3 to 4½ minutes or until melted. Continue as directed above.

NUTRITION INFORMATION PER SERVING

SERVING SIZE: 1 BAR		PERCENT U.S. RDA PER SERVING	
CALORIES	170	PROTEIN	2%
PROTEIN	2g	VITAMIN A	4%
CARBOHYDRATE	20g	VITAMIN C	*
FAT	9g	THIAMINE	*
CHOLESTEROL	8mg	RIBOFLAVIN	4%
SODIUM	115mg	NIACIN	*
POTASSIUM	70mg	CALCIUM	2%
		IRON	2%

*Contains less than 2% of the U.S. RDA of this nutrient.

Cookies
EXTRAORDINAIRE

Cookies
EXTRAORDINAIRE

Almost too pretty to eat...

Special occasions call for special
cookies! Teas, receptions, holiday
exchanges, party trays and gift
boxes all invite show-off shapes, rich flavors,
unique ingredients and imaginative decorative
touches. Yes, these recipes take a little more
time and skill than most drop and bar favorites,
but, oh, the spectacular results! Definitely worth
the effort.

We think you will take pleasure in these creative
recipes. Although some techniques may be new
to you, our precise instructions are designed in
detail to answer questions as you go. Cookie
making will be a breeze as you roll, press, shape
and decorate with professional ease and
confidence.

Beneficial to the success of many rolled, pressed
and molded cookies is a dough that is chilled
after mixing. This, along with a lightly-floured
work surface and hands, will help keep the
dough from sticking. When reusing a cookie
sheet for several bakings, use a cooled baking
sheet to prevent unattractive spreading and to
keep cookies "shapely." And when molding a
variety of shapes from the same dough, bake
like-shapes together for a uniform baking time.
A final note—don't risk the chance of breakage
when you move cookies from cookie sheet to
cooling rack. Let them cool slightly and then use
a wide spatula or turner to support the delicate
structure, unless the recipe indicates otherwise.

A candy-like fudge cookie that is easily prepared on the stovetop or in the microwave. Cookies can be made smaller and served in small paper cups for special occasions.

Raisin Nut Drops

2 cups sugar
1 cup half-and-half or evaporated milk
½ cup butter
6-oz. pkg. (1 cup) semi-sweet chocolate chips
1 cup graham cracker crumbs
1 cup raisins
1 cup chopped, toasted almonds*
¾ cup Pillsbury's BEST® All Purpose or Unbleached Flour
1 teaspoon vanilla extract

Grease cookie sheets. In saucepan over medium heat, combine sugar, half-and-half and butter. Bring to a full boil, stirring constantly. Boil 10 minutes, stirring occasionally. Remove from heat. Lightly spoon flour into measuring cup; level off. Add remaining ingredients; beat well. Let stand 5 minutes. Drop by rounded teaspoonfuls onto prepared cookie sheets. Cool. 4 dozen cookies.

▨ MICROWAVE DIRECTIONS: Grease cookie sheets. In 3-quart microwave-safe casserole, blend sugar and half-and-half. Add butter. Microwave on HIGH for 5 to 6 minutes or until mixture comes to a boil; stir. Microwave on MEDIUM for 10 minutes.** Continue as directed above.

TIPS: *To toast almonds, spread on cookie sheet; bake at 375°F. for 5 to 10 minutes or until light golden brown, stirring occasionally. Or, spread in thin layer in microwave-safe pie pan. Microwave on HIGH for 4 to 5 minutes or until light golden brown, stirring occasionally.

**If mixture has a curdled appearance after microwaving, beat with a wire whisk until smooth.

Shown on pages 58 and 59 —
L to R: Chocolate Almond Cups pg.68, Mandarin Orange Truffle Cookies pg.63, Walnut Wrap-Ups pg.65, Mint Blossoms pg.65, Raisin Nut Drops pg.61, Rum-Cherry Slices pg.61

NUTRITION INFORMATION PER SERVING

SERVING SIZE: 1 COOKIE		PERCENT U.S. RDA PER SERVING	
CALORIES	110	PROTEIN	*
PROTEIN	1g	VITAMIN A	*
CARBOHYDRATE	16g	VITAMIN C	*
FAT	5g	THIAMINE	*
CHOLESTEROL	6mg	RIBOFLAVIN	2%
SODIUM	35mg	NIACIN	*
POTASSIUM	70mg	CALCIUM	2%
		IRON	2%

*Contains less than 2% of the U.S. RDA of this nutrient.

This pretty, festive refrigerator ribbon cookie makes enough for a crowd.

Rum-Cherry Slices

1½ cups sugar
1 cup butter or margarine, softened
1 teaspoon vanilla
1 egg
2½ cups Pillsbury's BEST® All Purpose or Unbleached Flour
1½ teaspoons baking powder
½ teaspoon salt
½ cup finely chopped maraschino cherries, well drained
1 teaspoon rum extract
½ cup finely chopped raisins

Line 9x5-inch loaf pan with waxed paper. In a large bowl, beat sugar and butter until light and fluffy. Add vanilla and egg; blend well. Lightly spoon flour into measuring cup; level off. Stir in flour, baking powder and salt; mix well. Remove ⅓ of dough; stir in maraschino cherries; set aside. Stir rum extract and raisins into remaining ⅔ dough. Divide in half; spread ½ in bottom of prepared pan. Cover with cherry layer; top with remaining rum-raisin dough. Cover with waxed paper or plastic wrap; refrigerate overnight.

Heat oven to 375°F. Remove dough from pan; cut into thirds lengthwise. Cut into ¼-inch slices. Place 1 inch apart on ungreased cookie sheets. Bake at 375°F. for 4 to 6 minutes or until edges are light golden brown. 9 dozen cookies.

HIGH ALTITUDE—Above 3500 Feet: Increase flour to 2½ cups plus 2 tablespoons. Bake as directed above.

NUTRITION INFORMATION PER SERVING

SERVING SIZE: 1 COOKIE		PERCENT U.S. RDA PER SERVING	
CALORIES	40	PROTEIN	*
PROTEIN	0g	VITAMIN A	*
CARBOHYDRATE	6g	VITAMIN C	*
FAT	2g	THIAMINE	*
CHOLESTEROL	6mg	RIBOFLAVIN	*
SODIUM	30mg	NIACIN	*
POTASSIUM	10mg	CALCIUM	*
		IRON	*

*Contains less than 2% of the U.S. RDA of this nutrient.

These petite, colorful cookies are a "must" for special occasions.

Chocolate Pistachio Thumbprints ·

COOKIES

⅓	cup powdered sugar
1	cup butter or margarine, softened
1	teaspoon vanilla
¾	teaspoon almond extract
3½-oz.	pkg. instant pistachio pudding and pie filling mix
1	egg
2	cups Pillsbury's BEST® All Purpose or Unbleached Flour
½	cup miniature or regular semi-sweet chocolate chips
¾ to 1¼	cups finely chopped nuts

FILLING

1½	cups powdered sugar
2	tablespoons margarine or butter, softened
1	teaspoon vanilla
1 to 3	tablespoons milk

GLAZE

½	cup miniature or regular semi-sweet chocolate chips
2	teaspoons shortening

Heat oven to 350ºF. Lightly grease cookie sheets. In large bowl, beat ⅓ cup powdered sugar, 1 cup margarine, 1 teaspoon vanilla, almond extract, pudding mix and egg until well blended. Lightly spoon flour into measuring cup; level off. Stir in flour and ½ cup chocolate chips; mix well. If necessary, refrigerate dough 30 to 45 minutes for easier handling.

Shape dough into 1-inch balls; roll in nuts. Place 2 inches apart on prepared cookie sheets. With thumb, make imprint in center of each cookie. Bake at 350ºF. for 10 to 14 minutes or until edges are light golden brown. Cool 1 minute; remove from cookie sheets. Cool completely.

In small bowl, combine all filling ingredients until smooth. Spoon scant teaspoonful of filling into center of each cookie. In small saucepan over low heat, melt ½ cup chocolate chips with shortening, stirring constantly. Drizzle about ½ teaspoon glaze over each filled cookie. Allow filling and glaze to set before storing cookies. 3 to 4 dozen cookies. '

HIGH ALTITUDE—Above 3500 Feet: No change.

NUTRITION INFORMATION PER SERVING

SERVING SIZE: 1 COOKIE		PERCENT U.S. RDA PER SERVING	
CALORIES	120	PROTEIN	2%
PROTEIN	1g	VITAMIN A	2%
CARBOHYDRATE	12g	VITAMIN C	*
FAT	8g	THIAMINE	2%
CHOLESTEROL	15mg	RIBOFLAVIN	*
SODIUM	55mg	NIACIN	*
POTASSIUM	40mg	CALCIUM	2%
		IRON	2%

*Contains less than 2% of the U.S. RDA of this nutrient.

Decorator Frosting

2	egg whites
½	teaspoon cream of tartar
2	cups powdered sugar
¼ to ½	teaspoon vanilla, peppermint or mint extract
2 to 3	drops food coloring, if desired

In small bowl, beat egg whites with cream of tartar until soft peaks form. Gradually beat in powdered sugar and vanilla until frosting is smooth and stiff enough to hold firm peaks. Add food coloring. Keep frosting covered with damp paper towels while frosting cookies. 1¾ cups.

NUTRITION INFORMATION PER SERVING

SERVING SIZE: 1 TABLESPOON		PERCENT U.S. RDA PER SERVING	
CALORIES	30	PROTEIN	*
PROTEIN	0g	VITAMIN A	*
CARBOHYDRATE	7g	VITAMIN C	*
FAT	0g	THIAMINE	*
CHOLESTEROL	0mg	RIBOFLAVIN	*
SODIUM	0mg	NIACIN	*
POTASSIUM	0mg	CALCIUM	*
		IRON	*

*Contains less than 2% of the U.S. RDA of this nutrient.

To make these rich, tender sugar cookies, the delicate dough needs to be thoroughly chilled for easier handling. We recommend a well-floured pastry cloth and a stockinet-covered rolling pin to simplify rolling of the dough.

Extra Rich Sugar Cookies

- ½ cup sugar
- ½ cup butter, softened
- 1 tablespoon milk
- 1 teaspoon vanilla
- 1 egg
- 1¼ cups Pillsbury's BEST® All Purpose or Unbleached Flour
- 1 teaspoon cream of tartar
- ½ teaspoon baking soda
- ¼ teaspoon salt
  Decorator Frosting (recipe precedes)

In large bowl, beat sugar and butter until light and fluffy. Add milk, vanilla and egg; blend well. Lightly spoon flour into measuring cup; level off. Stir in flour, cream of tartar, baking soda and salt; mix well. Cover with plastic wrap; refrigerate 3 hours or until firm.

Heat oven to 425°F. Using stockinet-covered rolling pin and well-floured pastry cloth, roll dough, ⅓ at a time, to ⅛-inch thickness. Keep remaining dough refrigerated. Cut dough into desired shapes with lightly floured cookie cutters. Place 1 inch apart on ungreased cookie sheets. Repeat with remaining dough. Bake at 425°F. for 3 to 5 minutes or until edges are light golden brown. Immediately remove from cookie sheets. Frost with Decorator Frosting, if desired. 4 to 5 dozen cookies.

HIGH ALTITUDE—Above 3500 Feet: Increase flour to 1¼ cups plus 2 tablespoons. Bake as directed above.

NUTRITION INFORMATION PER SERVING

SERVING SIZE: 1 COOKIE		PERCENT U.S. RDA PER SERVING	
CALORIES	45	PROTEIN	*
PROTEIN	0g	VITAMIN A	*
CARBOHYDRATE	7g	VITAMIN C	*
FAT	2g	THIAMINE	*
CHOLESTEROL	8mg	RIBOFLAVIN	*
SODIUM	35mg	NIACIN	*
POTASSIUM	5mg	CALCIUM	*
		IRON	*

*Contains less than 2% of the U.S. RDA of this nutrient.

These creamy-textured truffles have a delicate, rich flavor without being overly sweet. The subtle orange-chocolate flavor is sure to please. Serve in decorative small paper cups for a special touch.

Mandarin Orange Truffle Cookies

- 11-oz. can mandarin oranges, drained
- 6-oz. pkg. (1 cup) semi-sweet chocolate chips
- ¼ cup whipping cream or evaporated milk
- 3 tablespoons butter
- 12-oz. box vanilla wafers, crushed (3 cups)
- ½ cup powdered sugar
- ½ cup ground almonds
- 2 tablespoons orange-flavored liqueur
- ¾ cup chocolate flavored sprinkles

In blender container or food processor bowl with metal blade, chop oranges very fine. In heavy saucepan, combine oranges, chocolate chips, cream and butter. Heat over low heat until chocolate melts, stirring constantly. Cook 5 minutes longer, stirring occasionally. Stir in cookie crumbs, sugar, almonds and liqueur. Refrigerate 30 minutes or until mixture is firm enough to handle. Shape into 1-inch balls; roll in chocolate sprinkles. To store, place in tightly covered container; refrigerate. 4½ dozen cookies.

■■ MICROWAVE DIRECTIONS: Chop oranges as directed above. In medium microwave-safe bowl, combine oranges, chocolate chips, cream and butter. Microwave on HIGH for 3 minutes or until chocolate melts; stirring twice during cooking. Continue as directed above.

NUTRITION INFORMATION PER SERVING

SERVING SIZE: 1 COOKIE		PERCENT U.S. RDA PER SERVING	
CALORIES	90	PROTEIN	*
PROTEIN	1g	VITAMIN A	*
CARBOHYDRATE	10g	VITAMIN C	2%
FAT	5g	THIAMINE	*
CHOLESTEROL	6mg	RIBOFLAVIN	*
SODIUM	25mg	NIACIN	*
POTASSIUM	35mg	CALCIUM	*
		IRON	*

*Contains less than 2% of the U.S. RDA of this nutrient.

These cookies are fun and easy to make with a pastry decorating bag. They will be a delightful conversation piece as well as delicious to eat.

Mint Blossoms

½ cup sugar
¾ cup butter or margarine, softened
1 egg
½ teaspoon mint extract
4 to 6 drops green food coloring
1¾ cups Pillsbury's BEST® All Purpose or Unbleached Flour
½ teaspoon baking soda
¼ teaspoon cream of tartar
¼ teaspoon salt
¼ cup butter or margarine, softened
1 tablespoon chocolate flavored syrup
¼ cup flour

In large bowl, beat sugar and ¾ cup butter until light and fluffy. Add egg, mint extract and food coloring; blend well. Lightly spoon flour into measuring cup; level off. Stir in 1¾ cups flour, baking soda, cream of tartar and salt. Knead dough into smooth ball. Wrap in plastic wrap; refrigerate 1 hour or until firm.

Meanwhile, in small bowl mix ¼ cup butter, chocolate syrup and ¼ cup flour with fork until well combined. Spoon mixture into decorating bag fitted with a small writing tube; set aside.

Heat oven to 375°F. Shape dough into ¼-inch balls. Place balls 2 inches apart on ungreased cookie sheets. With bottom of glass dipped in flour, flatten each ball into 1½-inch round. Pipe chocolate-flour mixture on top of each cookie in a blossom design by making two figure 8's perpendicular to each other. Bake at 375°F. for 5 to 7 minutes or until set. 6 dozen cookies.

HIGH ALTITUDE—Above 3500 Feet: No change.

NUTRITION INFORMATION PER SERVING

SERVING SIZE: 1 COOKIE		PERCENT U.S. RDA PER SERVING	
CALORIES	40	PROTEIN	*
PROTEIN	0g	VITAMIN A	*
CARBOHYDRATE	4g	VITAMIN C	*
FAT	3g	THIAMINE	*
CHOLESTEROL	10mg	RIBOFLAVIN	*
SODIUM	40mg	NIACIN	*
POTASSIUM	5mg	CALCIUM	*
		IRON	*

*Contains less than 2% of the U.S. RDA of this nutrient.

Mint Blossoms

A real cookie tray enhancer, the rich cream cheese pastry surrounds a moist walnut filling.

Walnut Wrap-Ups

PASTRY
1¼ cups Pillsbury's BEST® All Purpose or Unbleached Flour
3-oz. pkg. cream cheese, softened
½ cup butter, softened
FILLING
¾ cup ground walnuts
¼ cup sugar
2 tablespoons milk
½ teaspoon almond extract
1 egg, beaten
Powdered sugar

In medium bowl, place flour. Using pastry blender or fork, cut in cream cheese and butter until mixture resembles coarse crumbs. Knead until well blended. Shape dough into ball. Wrap in plastic wrap; refrigerate at least 1 hour or until firm.

Meanwhile, in small bowl combine ground walnuts, sugar, milk and almond extract; set aside. Heat oven to 375°F. On well-floured surface, roll dough into 14x8-inch rectangle; cut into 28 2-inch squares. Place rounded ½ teaspoonful of filling in center of each square. Pinch 2 opposite corners together over filling. Place on ungreased cookie sheets. Brush lightly with beaten egg. Bake at 375°F. for 10 to 12 minutes or until light golden in color. Immediately remove from cookie sheets; cool. Dust with powdered sugar. 28 cookies.

NUTRITION INFORMATION PER SERVING

SERVING SIZE: 1 COOKIE		PERCENT U.S. RDA PER SERVING	
CALORIES	80	PROTEIN	2%
PROTEIN	1g	VITAMIN A	2%
CARBOHYDRATE	7g	VITAMIN C	*
FAT	6g	THIAMINE	2%
CHOLESTEROL	20mg	RIBOFLAVIN	*
SODIUM	45mg	NIACIN	*
POTASSIUM	25mg	CALCIUM	*
		IRON	2%

*Contains less than 2% of the U.S. RDA of this nutrient.

Delicious jam-centered cookies with an eye-catching appearance.

Linzer Stars

½ cup sugar
½ cup butter, softened
1 tablespoon milk
1 teaspoon vanilla
1 egg
1¼ cups Pillsbury's BEST® All Purpose or Unbleached Flour
1 teaspoon cream of tartar
½ teaspoon baking soda
¼ teaspoon salt
Powdered sugar
½ cup cherry or red currant jelly

In large bowl, beat sugar and butter until light and fluffy. Add milk, vanilla and egg; blend well. Lightly spoon flour into measuring cup; level off. Stir in flour, cream of tartar, baking soda and salt; mix well. Cover with plastic wrap; refrigerate 3 hours or until firm.

Heat oven to 425°F. Using stockinet-covered rolling pin and well-floured pastry cloth, roll dough, ⅓ at a time, to ⅓-inch thickness. Keep remaining dough refrigerated. Cut with floured 3-inch star-shaped cookie cutter.* Using 1-inch round cookie cutter, cut hole in center of half of dough stars to form cookie tops. Place stars 1 inch apart on ungreased cookie sheets. Repeat with remaining dough. Bake at 425°F. for 3 to 5 minutes or until edges are light golden brown. Cool 1 minute; remove from cookie sheets. Cool completely. To assemble cookies, sprinkle powdered sugar over cookie tops. Spread ½ teaspoon of the jelly over each cookie bottom. Place sugar-topped cookie over jelly.
4 dozen sandwich cookies.

TIP: *A 2½-inch round cookie cutter may be substituted.

HIGH ALTITUDE—Above 3500 Feet: Increase flour to 1¼ cups plus 2 tablespoons. Bake as directed above.

NUTRITION INFORMATION PER SERVING

SERVING SIZE: 1 SANDWICH COOKIE		PERCENT U.S. RDA PER SERVING	
CALORIES	45	PROTEIN	*
PROTEIN	0g	VITAMIN A	*
CARBOHYDRATE	7g	VITAMIN C	*
FAT	2g	THIAMINE	*
CHOLESTEROL	10mg	RIBOFLAVIN	*
SODIUM	45mg	NIACIN	*
POTASSIUM	10mg	CALCIUM	*
		IRON	*

*Contains less than 2% of the U.S. RDA of this nutrient.

Linzer Stars

This heavenly cookie is just right to make a cookie tray complete.

Pastel Melt-Aways

COOKIES
½ cup powdered sugar
¾ cup butter or margarine, softened
1 cup Pillsbury's BEST® All Purpose or Unbleached Flour
½ cup cornstarch

GLAZE
1½ cups powdered sugar
1 teaspoon vanilla
1 tablespoon butter or margarine, softened
2 to 3 tablespoons milk
Food coloring

Heat oven to 325°F. In large bowl, beat powdered sugar and margarine until well blended. Lightly spoon flour into measuring cup; level off. Stir in flour and cornstarch; mix well. If necessary, refrigerate dough 30 minutes for easier handling.

Shape dough into ¾-inch balls. Place 2 inches apart on ungreased cookie sheet. Bake at 325°F. for 10 to 13 minutes or until edges are very light brown. Immediately remove from cookie sheets; cool completely.

In small bowl, combine all glaze ingredients except food coloring, adding enough milk for desired glaze consistency. Divide glaze into several small bowls; tint as desired with food coloring. Spoon glaze over cookies. Allow glaze to set completely before storing in tightly covered container.
3 to 4 dozen cookies.

NUTRITION INFORMATION PER SERVING

SERVING SIZE: 1 COOKIE		PERCENT U.S. RDA PER SERVING	
CALORIES	60	PROTEIN	*
PROTEIN	0g	VITAMIN A	2%
CARBOHYDRATE	7g	VITAMIN C	*
FAT	3g	THIAMINE	*
CHOLESTEROL	8mg	RIBOFLAVIN	*
SODIUM	30mg	NIACIN	*
POTASSIUM	5mg	CALCIUM	*
		IRON	*

*Contains less than 2% of the U.S. RDA of this nutrient.

Pastry-like dough is pressed into miniature muffin cups and filled with brownie nut filling.

Chocolate Almond Cups

PASTRY
½ cup sugar
¾ cup butter or margarine, softened
1 teaspoon vanilla
1¾ cups Pillsbury's BEST® All Purpose or Unbleached Flour
¼ teaspoon salt

FILLING
¾ cup almonds
6-oz. pkg. (1 cup) semi-sweet chocolate chips
2 eggs
½ cup sugar

Heat oven to 350°F. Grease bottoms and sides of miniature muffin cups or very small tart shells. In large bowl, beat sugar, butter and vanilla until light and fluffy. Lightly spoon flour into measuring cup; level off. Stir in flour and salt; mix well. Press rounded teaspoonfuls of dough in bottom and up sides of prepared pans.

Grind together almonds and chocolate chips; set aside. In small bowl, beat eggs and ½ cup sugar until thick and light colored. Fold in almond-chocolate mixture. Place a rounded teaspoonful of filling in each dough-lined cup. Bake at 350°F. for 15 to 20 minutes or until filling is set. Cool 15 minutes. Loosen tarts carefully; remove from pans.
3 dozen cookies.

HIGH ALTITUDE—Above 3500 Feet: Bake at 375°F. for 15 to 20 minutes.

NUTRITION INFORMATION PER SERVING

SERVING SIZE: 1 COOKIE		PERCENT U.S. RDA PER SERVING	
CALORIES	120	PROTEIN	2%
PROTEIN	2g	VITAMIN A	2%
CARBOHYDRATE	14g	VITAMIN C	*
FAT	7g	THIAMINE	2%
CHOLESTEROL	25mg	RIBOFLAVIN	2%
SODIUM	55mg	NIACIN	2%
POTASSIUM	50mg	CALCIUM	2%
		IRON	2%

*Contains less than 2% of the U.S. RDA of this nutrient.

This elegant cookie has a crisp buttery base with a coconut macaroon topping and chocolate glaze.

Coconut Diamond Gems

COOKIES
¾ cup sugar
¾ cup butter or margarine, softened
1 teaspoon vanilla
1 egg yolk
1½ cups Pillsbury's BEST® All Purpose or Unbleached Flour
½ teaspoon cinnamon
¼ teaspoon salt
TOPPING
2 cups coconut
½ cup powdered sugar
1 egg white, slightly beaten
1 tablespoon water
½ teaspoon vanilla
½ cup chopped nuts
GLAZE
3 oz. (3 squares) semi-sweet chocolate
1 teaspoon shortening

In large bowl, beat ¾ cup sugar, butter and 1 teaspoon vanilla until light and fluffy. Add egg yolk; blend well. Lightly spoon flour into measuring cup; level off. Stir in flour, cinnamon and salt; mix well. Cover with plastic wrap; refrigerate 1 hour or until firm.

Heat oven to 375°F. Lightly dust large cookie sheet with flour. On cookie sheet, roll half of dough to 10½x8½-inch rectangle. With tip of sharp knife, score long edge of dough forming 7 (1½-inch wide) strips. Score eight diagonal markings to form 32 diamond-shaped pieces. In small bowl, combine coconut, powdered sugar, egg white, water, ½ teaspoon vanilla and nuts; mix well. Place 1 level teaspoonful of coconut mixture in center of each diamond. Repeat with remaining dough. Bake at 375°F. for 8 to 11 minutes or until lightly browned. Cut completely through score marks to make diamonds. Remove from cookie sheet; cool completely.

In small saucepan over very low heat, melt chocolate and shortening, stirring constantly. Drizzle over coconut mixture. 64 cookies.

HIGH ALTITUDE—Above 3500 Feet: No change.

NUTRITION INFORMATION PER SERVING

SERVING SIZE: 1 COOKIE		PERCENT U.S. RDA PER SERVING	
CALORIES	70	PROTEIN	*
PROTEIN	1g	VITAMIN A	*
CARBOHYDRATE	7g	VITAMIN C	*
FAT	4g	THIAMINE	*
CHOLESTEROL	10mg	RIBOFLAVIN	*
SODIUM	30mg	NIACIN	*
POTASSIUM	25mg	CALCIUM	*
		IRON	*

*Contains less than 2% of the U.S. RDA of this nutrient.

A colorful, fancy, chewy cookie with an Italian heritage. Store between sheets of waxed paper in a tightly covered container.

Florentines

⅓ cup butter
⅓ cup honey
¼ cup sugar
2 tablespoons milk
⅔ cup Pillsbury's BEST® All Purpose or Unbleached Flour
1½ cups assorted candied fruit, coarsely chopped

Heat oven to 325°F. Generously grease cookie sheets. In medium saucepan, melt butter. Remove from heat; stir in honey, sugar and milk. Lightly spoon flour into measuring cup; level off. Stir in flour. Cook over medium heat until mixture thickens slightly, about 3 to 6 minutes, stirring constantly. Remove from heat; stir in candied fruit. Drop mixture by teaspoonfuls 2 inches apart on prepared cookie sheets. Bake at 325°F. for 10 to 12 minutes or until edges are light golden brown. Cool 2 minutes; carefully remove from cookie sheets. 2½ dozen cookies.

HIGH ALTITUDE—Above 3500 Feet: Increase flour to ⅔ cup plus 1 tablespoon. Bake as directed above.

NUTRITION INFORMATION PER SERVING

SERVING SIZE: 1 COOKIE		PERCENT U.S. RDA PER SERVING	
CALORIES	70	PROTEIN	*
PROTEIN	0g	VITAMIN A	*
CARBOHYDRATE	14g	VITAMIN C	2%
FAT	2g	THIAMINE	2%
CHOLESTEROL	6mg	RIBOFLAVIN	*
SODIUM	30mg	NIACIN	*
POTASSIUM	50mg	CALCIUM	*
		IRON	*

*Contains less than 2% of the U.S. RDA of this nutrient.

This recipe transforms meringue into extraordinary pecan cookies with very little effort. Store the cookies tightly covered, because egg white cookies dry out quickly.

Pecan Puff Balls

- 2 egg whites
- ⅛ teaspoon cream of tartar
- 2 cups powdered sugar
- 1½ cups finely chopped pecans
- ½ teaspoon grated orange peel

Heat oven to 325°F. Grease cookie sheets. In small bowl, beat egg whites and cream of tartar until soft peaks form. Gradually add sugar; continue beating an additional 5 minutes or until mixture is very stiff. Remove ⅓ of mixture; set aside.

Fold nuts and orange peel into remaining meringue. Drop by scant teaspoonfuls 2 inches apart onto prepared cookie sheets. Make a small indentation in center of each cookie. Fill each with a rounded half teaspoon of reserved meringue. Bake at 325°F. for 13 to 16 minutes or until meringue is delicate brown. Immediately remove from cookie sheets. 4 dozen cookies.

HIGH ALTITUDE—Above 3500 Feet: No change.

NUTRITION INFORMATION PER SERVING

SERVING SIZE: 1 COOKIE		PERCENT U.S. RDA PER SERVING	
CALORIES	40	PROTEIN	*
PROTEIN	0g	VITAMIN A	*
CARBOHYDRATE	5g	VITAMIN C	*
FAT	2g	THIAMINE	2%
CHOLESTEROL	0mg	RIBOFLAVIN	*
SODIUM	0mg	NIACIN	*
POTASSIUM	15mg	CALCIUM	*
		IRON	*

*Contains less than 2% of the U.S. RDA of this nutrient.

Pineapple Strip

A distinctive looking strip cookie with an irresistible pineapple filling.

Pineapple Strips

PASTRY

½ cup sugar
½ cup firmly packed brown sugar
½ cup butter or margarine, softened
3-oz. pkg. cream cheese, softened
1 teaspoon vanilla
1 egg
2 cups Pillsbury's BEST® All Purpose or Unbleached Flour
½ teaspoon baking powder
¼ teaspoon salt

FILLING

20-oz. can crushed pineapple, drained, reserving liquid
¼ cup sugar
2 tablespoons cornstarch
⅛ teaspoon mace or nutmeg

GLAZE

1 cup powdered sugar
½ teaspoon vanilla
1 to 2 tablespoons reserved pineapple liquid
2 tablespoons sliced almonds

In large bowl, beat ½ cup sugar, brown sugar, butter and cream cheese until light and fluffy. Add vanilla and egg; blend well. Lightly spoon flour into measuring cup; level off. Stir in flour, baking powder and salt; mix well. Wrap dough in plastic wrap; refrigerate 2 hours or overnight.

In small saucepan over medium heat, cook ⅓ cup reserved pineapple liquid and all filling ingredients until thickened, stirring constantly. Remove from heat; cool.

Heat oven to 350°F. On well-floured surface, roll out dough, ¼ at a time, to 12x6-inch rectangle. Spread scant ½ cup of filling lengthwise down center of rectangle. Fold each lengthwise edge of dough over filling just so the two edges meet. Place on ungreased cookie sheet. Repeat with remaining dough, placing 2 strips on each cookie sheet. Bake at 350°F. for 20 to 24 minutes or until light golden brown. Cool on cookie sheet.

In small bowl, combine all glaze ingredients except almonds, adding enough pineapple juice for glaze consistency. Drizzle evenly over strips.

Sprinkle with sliced almonds; cut each roll into 12 slices. Store in airtight container in refrigerator.
4 dozen cookies.

HIGH ALTITUDE—Above 3500 Feet: Increase flour to 2½ cups. Bake as directed above.

NUTRITION INFORMATION PER SERVING

SERVING SIZE: 1 COOKIE		PERCENT U.S. RDA PER SERVING	
CALORIES	80	PROTEIN	*
PROTEIN	1g	VITAMIN A	2%
CARBOHYDRATE	14g	VITAMIN C	*
FAT	3g	THIAMINE	2%
CHOLESTEROL	10mg	RIBOFLAVIN	*
SODIUM	40mg	NIACIN	*
POTASSIUM	35mg	CALCIUM	*
		IRON	2%

*Contains less than 2% of the U.S. RDA of this nutrient.

You'll be delighted with this attractive and popular blend of cherries and chocolate.

Cherry Chocolate Kisses

1 cup powdered sugar
1 cup butter or margarine, softened
2 teaspoons maraschino cherry juice
½ teaspoon almond extract
Few drops red food coloring
2¼ cups Pillsbury's BEST® All Purpose or Unbleached Flour
½ teaspoon salt
½ cup maraschino cherries, drained, chopped
48 chocolate kisses, unwrapped

Heat oven to 350°F. In large bowl, combine powdered sugar, margarine, cherry juice, almond extract and food coloring; blend well. Lightly spoon flour into measuring cup; level off. Stir in flour and salt; mix well. Stir in cherries. Shape dough into 1-inch balls. Place 2 inches apart on ungreased cookie sheets. Bake at 350°F. for 8 to 10 minutes or until edges are light golden brown. Immediately top each cookie with chocolate kiss. Remove from cookie sheets. 4 dozen cookies.

HIGH ALTITUDE—Above 3500 Feet: No change.

NUTRITION INFORMATION PER SERVING

SERVING SIZE: 1 COOKIE		PERCENT U.S. RDA PER SERVING	
CALORIES	90	PROTEIN	*
PROTEIN	1g	VITAMIN A	2%
CARBOHYDRATE	10g	VITAMIN C	*
FAT	5g	THIAMINE	2%
CHOLESTEROL	10mg	RIBOFLAVIN	2%
SODIUM	65mg	NIACIN	*
POTASSIUM	30mg	CALCIUM	2%
		IRON	*

*Contains less than 2% of the U.S. RDA of this nutrient.

A creamy, flavorful, extra-special filling is sandwiched between crisp, tender cookie rounds.

Vanilla Sandwich Cookies

COOKIES
- ½ cup sugar
- ½ cup butter, softened
- 1 tablespoon milk
- 1 teaspoon vanilla
- 1 egg
- 1¼ cups Pillsbury's BEST® All Purpose or Unbleached Flour
- 1 teaspoon cream of tartar
- ½ teaspoon baking soda
- ¼ teaspoon salt
- Sugar

FILLING
- 2 tablespoons butter
- 1⅓ cups powdered sugar
- ⅓ cup unsweetened cocoa
- 4 teaspoons hot water
- 2 to 3 tablespoons coffee-flavored liqueur

In large bowl, beat sugar and ½ cup butter until light and fluffy. Add milk, vanilla and egg; blend well. Lightly spoon flour into measuring cup; level off. Stir in flour, cream of tartar, baking soda and salt; mix well. Cover with plastic wrap; refrigerate 3 hours or until firm.

Heat oven to 425°F. Using stockinet-covered rolling pin and well-floured pastry cloth, roll dough, ⅓ at a time, to ⅛-inch thickness. Keep remaining dough refrigerated. Cut with floured 1½-inch round cookie cutter. Sprinkle tops with sugar. Place 1 inch apart on ungreased cookie sheets. Repeat with remaining dough. Bake at 425°F. for 3 to 5 minutes or until edges are light golden brown. Immediately remove from cookie sheets; cool completely.

In small bowl, combine all filling ingredients, adding enough liqueur for desired frosting consistency. Spread rounded ½ teaspoon filling between 2 cooled cookies. 5 dozen sandwich cookies.

HIGH ALTITUDE—Above 3500 Feet: Increase flour to 1¼ cups plus 2 tablespoons. Bake as directed above.

Roll-out lemon cookies covered with "twinkling" sugar crystals.

Lemon Snowflake Cookies

- 1 cup sugar
- 1 cup butter or margarine, softened
- 3 tablespoons milk
- 2 teaspoons grated lemon peel
- 1 egg
- 3 cups Pillsbury's BEST® All Purpose or Unbleached Flour
- 1½ teaspoons baking powder
- ½ teaspoon salt
- Pearl sugar, crushed sugar cubes or granulated sugar

Heat oven to 400°F. In large bowl, beat 1 cup sugar and margarine until light and fluffy. Add milk, lemon peel and egg; blend well. Lightly spoon flour into measuring cup; level off. Stir in flour, baking powder and salt; mix well. If necessary, refrigerate dough 1 to 2 hours for easier handling.

On lightly floured surface, roll dough, ⅓ at a time, to ⅛-inch thickness. Cut with lightly floured 2-inch snowflake cookie cutter. Place 1 inch apart on ungreased cookie sheets. Sprinkle with sugar. Bake at 400°F. for 6 to 8 minutes or until edges are light golden brown. Immediately remove from cookie sheets. 15 dozen cookies.

HIGH ALTITUDE—Above 3500 Feet: No change.

Melt Away Butter Fingers and Variations

Here's a favorite by many different names. Scandinavians know it as Butterball or Ciffarlis, the Russians as Teacakes and the Mexicans as Wedding Cakes. The shape may be in a ball, a crescent or in a log as used here. The proportion of ingredients may vary slightly and they may or may not be rolled in powdered sugar while still warm. We have created variations dipped in chocolate and nuts or with chocolate chips in the dough.

Melt Away Butter Fingers

2 cups Pillsbury's BEST® All
    Purpose or Unbleached Flour
½ cup powdered sugar
⅛ teaspoon salt
1 cup butter or margarine
1 teaspoon vanilla
1 cup finely chopped walnuts
    Powdered sugar

Heat oven to 400°F. Lightly spoon flour into measuring cup; level off. In large bowl, combine flour, powdered sugar and salt. Using pastry blender or fork, cut in butter until mixture resembles coarse crumbs. Add vanilla and nuts; mix with hands to form a smooth dough. Using about 1 tablespoon dough, shape into 2½-inch fingers. Place on ungreased cookie sheets. Bake at 400°F. for 5 to 7 minutes or until set and light golden brown. Cool 1 minute; remove from cookie sheets. Carefully roll in powdered sugar; cool. Store in tightly covered container. 5 dozen cookies.

Nutty Chocolate Butter Fingers: Omit walnuts from above recipe. Shape and bake dough as directed above except using about 1 teaspoon of dough. Do not roll in powdered sugar. In small saucepan over very low heat, melt ½ cup chocolate chips and 1 teaspoon margarine or butter; cool slightly. Spread ½ cup finely chopped pistachio nuts on waxed paper. Dip ends of Butter Fingers into chocolate mixture, then into nuts. Let stand on wire racks until chocolate is firm. 5 dozen cookies.

Chocolate Chip Butterballs: Prepare dough as directed above, substituting 1 cup miniature semi-sweet chocolate chips for 1 cup finely chopped walnuts. Shape into 1-inch balls. Place 1 inch apart on ungreased cookie sheets. Bake at 325°F. for 14 to 17 minutes or until firm to the touch but not brown. DO NOT OVERBAKE. Immediately remove from cookie sheets. Roll in powdered sugar; cool. 5 dozen cookies.

NUTRITION INFORMATION PER SERVING

SERVING SIZE: 1 COOKIE		PERCENT U.S. RDA PER SERVING	
CALORIES	60	PROTEIN	*
PROTEIN	1g	VITAMIN A	2%
CARBOHYDRATE	4g	VITAMIN C	*
FAT	4g	THIAMINE	2%
CHOLESTEROL	8mg	RIBOFLAVIN	*
SODIUM	35mg	NIACIN	*
POTASSIUM	15mg	CALCIUM	*
		IRON	*

*Contains less than 2% of the U.S. RDA of this nutrient.

Cookies
AROUND THE WORLD

Cookies
AROUND THE WORLD

A sweet summit with foreign flair...

As much as we all appreciate convenience cooking for day to day practicality, we still savor the more unique recipes which remind us of our heritage. Oh, how we treasure those hand-me-downs that "came over" with another generation and are still enjoyed today. And, what a delight it is to be able to duplicate in our own kitchen a cookie that captured our fancy while on a foreign adventure.

It is a tribute to the recipes in this chapter that they have endured for so long and traveled so well from old world to new. Although vastly different in flavor and appearance, all share common traits. Ingredients are rich and high-quality, often featuring buttery, nut-sparked doughs. And, each has a distinctive culinary personality, whether it be method of preparation using a special iron, press or rolling pin, the unique shaping or the unusual presentation that makes it immediately recognizable as a cookie tray stand-out.

Please refer to our cookie-baking tips at the front of the book for guidance on chopping and storing nuts, melting chocolate and choosing ingredients. We feel you will find the suggestions particularly helpful with these international creations. If the recipe calls for toasting nuts, instructions are included in a tip for your convenience. And, each recipe offers a doneness description, so that your cookies will be baked to perfection.

These German "picture cookies" must dry overnight before baking. The dough is pressed into special molds, or designs are rolled on with a special springerle rolling pin. The cookies contain anise oil which gives them their distinctive licorice flavor. Storing the baked cookies for several weeks helps develop this flavor.

Springerle

4	eggs
2	cups sugar
4 to 6	drops anise oil or ½ to 1 teaspoon anise extract
3½	cups Pillsbury's BEST® All Purpose or Unbleached Flour
1	teaspoon baking powder
¼	teaspoon salt

Lightly grease cookie sheets. In large bowl, beat eggs on highest speed until very thick, about 3 to 4 minutes. Gradually beat in sugar; continue beating for 15 minutes. Beat in anise oil. Lightly spoon flour into measuring cup; level off. Stir in remaining ingredients. Cover with plastic wrap; refrigerate 1 hour.

On well-floured surface, roll dough into rectangular shape, ½-inch thick, the same width as springerle rolling pin. Roll designs in dough. Cut cookies along design lines and place on prepared cookie sheets. Cover with cloth; let stand in cool place overnight.

Heat oven to 375°F. Place cookies in oven; immediately decrease temperature to 300°F. Bake 20 to 25 minutes or until set. Immediately remove from cookie sheets. Store in tightly covered container several weeks before using. 4 dozen cookies.

TIP: If springerle mold is used, roll dough ½-inch thick and press floured mold into dough; lift off and cut along design lines.

HIGH ALTITUDE—Above 3500 Feet: No change.

NUTRITION INFORMATION PER SERVING

SERVING SIZE: 1 COOKIE		PERCENT U.S. RDA PER SERVING	
CALORIES	70	PROTEIN	2%
PROTEIN	1g	VITAMIN A	*
CARBOHYDRATE	15g	VITAMIN C	*
FAT	1g	THIAMINE	4%
CHOLESTEROL	25mg	RIBOFLAVIN	2%
SODIUM	25mg	NIACIN	2%
POTASSIUM	20mg	CALCIUM	2%
		IRON	2%

*Contains less than 2% of the U.S. RDA of this nutrient.

Shown on pages 74 and 75 — Springerle

Authentic Chinese almond cookies would contain rice flour. This pleasing version can be topped with a whole blanched or unblanched almond.

Chinese Almond Cakes

¾	cup sugar
¾	cup butter or margarine, softened
2	tablespoons water
1	teaspoon almond extract
1	egg
2½	cups Pillsbury's BEST® All Purpose or Unbleached Flour
1	teaspoon baking powder
¼	teaspoon salt
½	cup whole almonds

Heat oven to 350°F. In large bowl, beat sugar, butter, water, almond extract and egg until well blended. Lightly spoon flour into measuring cup; level off. Stir in flour, baking powder and salt; mix well. Shape into 1-inch balls. Place 2 inches apart on ungreased cookie sheets. Flatten balls slightly with bottom of glass dipped in sugar; press whole almond firmly in center of each cookie. Bake at 350°F. for 7 to 10 minutes or until firm to the touch but not brown. DO NOT OVERBAKE. Immediately remove from cookie sheets. 5 dozen cookies.

HIGH ALTITUDE—Above 3500 Feet: No change.

NUTRITION INFORMATION PER SERVING

SERVING SIZE: 1 COOKIE		PERCENT U.S. RDA PER SERVING	
CALORIES	60	PROTEIN	*
PROTEIN	1g	VITAMIN A	*
CARBOHYDRATE	7g	VITAMIN C	*
FAT	3g	THIAMINE	2%
CHOLESTEROL	10mg	RIBOFLAVIN	*
SODIUM	40mg	NIACIN	*
POTASSIUM	15mg	CALCIUM	*
		IRON	*

*Contains less than 2% of the U.S. RDA of this nutrient.

An interesting cookie with a sugar cookie base, almond-sour cream filling and a meringue top! They are called Smettanich in Russian.

Russian Sour Cream Tarts

COOKIES
1¼ cups Pillsbury's BEST® All
      Purpose or Unbleached Flour
¼ cup sugar
¼ teaspoon salt
½ cup butter
1 egg yolk, slightly beaten
FILLING
1¼ cups ground blanched almonds
2 tablespoons powdered sugar
3 tablespoons dairy sour cream
2 tablespoons peach or apricot
    preserves
1 egg
MERINGUE
2 egg whites
¼ cup sugar

Heat oven to 350°F. Lightly spoon flour into measuring cup; level off. In large bowl, combine flour, sugar and salt. Using pastry blender or fork, cut in butter until mixture resembles coarse crumbs. Add egg yolk; knead until smooth dough forms, adding a few drops of ice water if needed. On lightly floured surface, roll dough ¼-inch thick; cut with floured, small scalloped cookie cutter. Place 1 inch apart on ungreased cookie sheets.

In small bowl, combine ground almonds and powdered sugar. Add sour cream, preserves and egg; mix well. Top each cookie with 1 rounded teaspoon of filling; carefully spread over cookie. In small bowl, beat egg whites until soft peaks form; gradually add sugar, beating until stiff peaks form. Top each cookie with teaspoonful of meringue, swirling top. Bake at 350°F. for 10 to 12 minutes or until meringue is delicate brown. Immediately remove from cookie sheets; cool. Store loosely covered.
3 dozen cookies.

HIGH ALTITUDE—Above 3500 Feet: Decrease sugar in meringue to 3 tablespoons. Bake at 325°F. for 10 to 15 minutes.

NUTRITION INFORMATION PER SERVING

SERVING SIZE: 1 COOKIE		PERCENT U.S. RDA PER SERVING	
CALORIES	90	PROTEIN	2%
PROTEIN	2g	VITAMIN A	2%
CARBOHYDRATE	8g	VITAMIN C	*
FAT	6g	THIAMINE	2%
CHOLESTEROL	25mg	RIBOFLAVIN	4%
SODIUM	45mg	NIACIN	2%
POTASSIUM	50mg	CALCIUM	2%
		IRON	2%

*Contains less than 2% of the U.S. RDA of this nutrient.

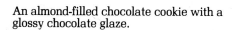

An almond-filled chocolate cookie with a glossy chocolate glaze.

Austrian Chocolate Balls

COOKIES

    2 oz. (2 squares) unsweetened
        chocolate, cut-up
    ⅓ cup margarine or butter
    1 cup sugar
    ½ teaspoon almond extract
    1 egg
    1 egg yolk
    1⅓ cups Pillsbury's BEST® All
        Purpose or Unbleached
        Flour
    ½ cup finely chopped almonds
GLAZE
    1 oz. (1 square) unsweetened
        chocolate, cut-up
    1 tablespoon margarine or
        butter
    ¼ teaspoon almond extract
    1 cup powdered sugar
    2 to 3 tablespoons milk

Heat oven to 350°F. In medium saucepan, melt 2 oz. chocolate and ⅓ cup margarine over low heat. Remove from heat. Stir in sugar, almond extract, egg and egg yolk; blend well. Lightly spoon flour into measuring cup; level off. Gradually stir in flour and nuts; mix well. Shape into 1-inch balls. Place on ungreased cookie sheets. Bake at 350°F. for 7 to 10 minutes or until firm to the touch. DO NOT OVERBAKE. Immediately remove from cookie sheets; cool.

In small saucepan over low heat, melt 1 oz. chocolate with 1 tablespoon margarine, stirring constantly. Remove from heat. Stir in remaining ingredients, adding enough milk for desired glaze consistency; blend well. Dip tops of cookies into glaze. Allow glaze to set completely before storing in tightly covered container. 3 dozen cookies.

NUTRITION INFORMATION PER SERVING

SERVING SIZE: 1 COOKIE		PERCENT U.S. RDA PER SERVING	
CALORIES	90	PROTEIN	2%
PROTEIN	1g	VITAMIN A	2%
CARBOHYDRATE	13g	VITAMIN C	*
FAT	4g	THIAMINE	2%
CHOLESTEROL	15mg	RIBOFLAVIN	2%
SODIUM	25mg	NIACIN	*
POTASSIUM	40mg	CALCIUM	*
		IRON	2%

*Contains less than 2% of the U.S. RDA of this nutrient.

Poppy seed fillings from scratch have long been a Bohemian trademark. With these bars we can have Old World flavor with present day convenience.

Bohemian Poppy Seed Bars

CRUST

    1¼ cups Pillsbury's BEST® All
        Purpose or Unbleached
        Flour
    ½ cup powdered sugar
    1 teaspoon baking powder
    ¼ teaspoon salt
    ½ cup butter
    ½ cup chopped, slivered
        almonds
    ½ teaspoon almond extract
    1 egg, beaten
FILLING
    12½-oz. can prepared poppy seed,
        prune or apricot filling

Heat oven to 350°F. Lightly spoon flour into measuring cup; level off. In medium bowl, combine flour, powdered sugar, baking powder and salt. Using pastry blender or fork, cut in butter until mixture resembles coarse crumbs. Stir in nuts. Add almond extract and egg; mix well. (Mixture will still be crumbly.) Press half of crumb mixture in ungreased 9-inch square pan. Spread poppy seed filling evenly over crust. Sprinkle remaining crumb mixture on top. Press down gently. Bake at 350°F. for 30 to 35 minutes or until top is light golden brown. Cool completely. Cut into bars. 25 bars.

HIGH ALTITUDE—Above 3500 Feet: No change.

NUTRITION INFORMATION PER SERVING

SERVING SIZE: 1 BAR		PERCENT U.S. RDA PER SERVING	
CALORIES	120	PROTEIN	2%
PROTEIN	2g	VITAMIN A	2%
CARBOHYDRATE	14g	VITAMIN C	*
FAT	6g	THIAMINE	4%
CHOLESTEROL	20mg	RIBOFLAVIN	2%
SODIUM	80mg	NIACIN	2%
POTASSIUM	30mg	CALCIUM	8%
		IRON	4%

*Contains less than 2% of the U.S. RDA of this nutrient.

Reminiscent of Hungarian pastry, this dough is light and flaky because of the cottage cheese curds dispersed in the dough. Add a moist, flavorful filling and you'll enjoy cookies that are irresistible.

Apricot-Date Pockets

PASTRY
- ⅓ cup powdered sugar
- ¾ cup butter or margarine, softened
- ⅔ cup creamed cottage cheese
- ½ teaspoon vanilla
- 1¾ cups Pillsbury's BEST® All Purpose or Unbleached Flour
- ⅛ teaspoon salt

FILLING
- ⅓ cup finely chopped dates
- ⅓ cup finely chopped dried apricots
- ¼ cup sugar
- 2 tablespoons water
- ½ teaspoon vanilla

- 1 egg, beaten

In large bowl, beat powdered sugar and butter until light and fluffy. Add cottage cheese and vanilla; blend well. Lightly spoon flour into measuring cup; level off. Stir in flour and salt. Knead into a ball. Wrap in plastic wrap; refrigerate 2 hours or until firm.

In small saucepan over medium-high heat, combine all filling ingredients except vanilla; cook until thickened, stirring occasionally. Remove from heat; stir in vanilla. Cool.

Heat oven to 375°F. On lightly floured surface roll out dough, ½ at a time, to ⅛-inch thickness. Keep remaining dough refrigerated. Cut dough with a floured 3-inch round cookie cutter. Cut a small star shape for each round. Place rounds ½ inch apart on ungreased cookie sheets. Place ½ teaspoon filling on half of each dough round. Brush edges with beaten egg; fold dough over filling to form pocket. With floured fork firmly press edges to seal. Top pocket with dough star. Brush top of pocket with beaten egg. Repeat with remaining dough. Bake at 375°F. for 9 to 13 minutes or until golden brown. Immediately remove from cookie sheets. 2½ dozen cookies.

HIGH ALTITUDE—Above 3500 Feet: No change.

NUTRITION INFORMATION PER SERVING

SERVING SIZE: 1 COOKIE		PERCENT U.S. RDA PER SERVING	
CALORIES	90	PROTEIN	2%
PROTEIN	2g	VITAMIN A	6%
CARBOHYDRATE	11g	VITAMIN C	*
FAT	5g	THIAMINE	2%
CHOLESTEROL	20mg	RIBOFLAVIN	2%
SODIUM	80mg	NIACIN	2%
POTASSIUM	50mg	CALCIUM	2%
		IRON	2%

*Contains less than 2% of the U.S. RDA of this nutrient.

Hazelnuts, also called filberts, are widely used in the middle European countries. They are less oily than walnuts or pecans. To bring out their best flavor, they should be toasted as in these superb bars.

Bavarian Hazelnut Dream Bars

CRUST
1 cup Pillsbury's BEST® All Purpose or Unbleached Flour
¼ cup sugar
⅛ teaspoon salt
½ cup butter

FILLING
½ cup orange marmalade
½ cup firmly packed brown sugar
2 eggs
¼ teaspoon vanilla
1 cup coarsely chopped, toasted hazelnuts (filberts)*
1 cup coconut
½ teaspoon baking powder
⅛ teaspoon salt
Powdered sugar, if desired

Heat oven to 350°F. Lightly spoon flour into measuring cup; level off. In medium bowl, combine flour, sugar and salt. Using pastry blender or fork, cut in butter until mixture resembles coarse crumbs. Press mixture in ungreased 9-inch square pan. Bake at 350°F. for 20 to 22 minutes or until lightly browned. Cool 10 minutes on wire rack. Spread marmalade over crust. In small bowl, beat brown sugar, eggs and vanilla until well blended and light in color. Stir in remaining ingredients except powdered sugar; mix well. Carefully spoon mixture over preserves. Bake at 350°F. for 25 to 30 minutes or until deep golden brown. Cool completely; sprinkle with powdered sugar. Cut into bars, squares or triangles. 25 bars.

Bavarian Hazelnut Dream Bars

This cookie, called cucas (koo-kahs), is native to the central western part of Colombia. They use panela, a sweetener made from cane sugar, instead of the dark brown sugar used in this recipe, but the result is a similar, strong-flavored, chewy cookie. On special occasions this cookie is frosted.

Colombian Dark Sugar Cookies

COOKIES
2¼ cups firmly packed dark
　　　brown sugar
½ cup butter, softened
2 eggs
2¼ cups Pillsbury's BEST® All
　　　Purpose or Unbleached Flour
½ teaspoon baking powder

GLAZE
5 teaspoons butter
¼ teaspoon instant coffee
　　　granules or crystals
2 tablespoons milk
¼ teaspoon vanilla
1 cup powdered sugar

Heat oven to 325°F. Lightly grease cookie sheets. In large bowl, beat brown sugar and butter until well blended. Add eggs; blend well. Lightly spoon flour into measuring cup; level off. Stir in flour and baking powder; mix well.

On lightly floured surface, roll dough to ¼-inch thickness. With pizza cutter, pastry wheel or sharp knife, cut dough into 1½x2½-inch rectangles. Place 1 inch apart on prepared cookie sheets. Generously prick tops of cookies with fork. Bake at 325°F. for 11 to 12 minutes or until set. Immediately remove from cookie sheets. Cool.

In small bowl, combine butter, coffee, milk and vanilla; beat well. Stir in powdered sugar; mix well. Drizzle over each cookie. 5 dozen cookies.

HIGH ALTITUDE—Above 3500 Feet: Increase flour to 2½ cups. Bake as directed above.

TIP: *To toast hazelnuts, spread on cookie sheet; bake at 350°F. for 10 to 12 minutes or until light golden brown, stirring occasionally.

HIGH ALTITUDE—Above 3500 Feet: No change.

NUTRITION INFORMATION PER SERVING

SERVING SIZE: 1 BAR		PERCENT U.S. RDA PER SERVING	
CALORIES	140	PROTEIN	2%
PROTEIN	2g	VITAMIN A	2%
CARBOHYDRATE	17g	VITAMIN C	*
FAT	8g	THIAMINE	4%
CHOLESTEROL	30mg	RIBOFLAVIN	2%
SODIUM	70mg	NIACIN	*
POTASSIUM	60mg	CALCIUM	2%
		IRON	4%

*Contains less than 2% of the U.S. RDA of this nutrient.

NUTRITION INFORMATION PER SERVING

SERVING SIZE: 1 COOKIE		PERCENT U.S. RDA PER SERVING	
CALORIES	70	PROTEIN	*
PROTEIN	1g	VITAMIN A	*
CARBOHYDRATE	13g	VITAMIN C	*
FAT	2g	THIAMINE	2%
CHOLESTEROL	15mg	RIBOFLAVIN	*
SODIUM	25mg	NIACIN	*
POTASSIUM	40mg	CALCIUM	2%
		IRON	2%

*Contains less than 2% of the U.S. RDA of this nutrient.

A cookie in the shape of a pretzel might lead you to believe it is only for children; however, the delicate almond flavoring will please all ages.

Edelweiss Almond Pretzel Cookies

1 cup powdered sugar
¾ cup butter or margarine, softened
2 eggs, separated
1 egg
¼ cup finely ground almonds
½ teaspoon almond extract
2¼ cups Pillsbury's BEST® All Purpose or Unbleached Flour
Pearl sugar, crushed sugar cubes or granulated sugar

In large bowl, beat butter and powdered sugar until light and fluffy. Add 2 egg yolks and 1 egg, one at a time, beating well after each addition. Add almonds and extract; blend well. Lightly spoon flour into measuring cup; level off. Stir in flour; mix well. Form dough into ball; wrap in plastic wrap. Refrigerate about 2 hours or until firm.

Heat oven to 400°F. Grease cookie sheets. Divide dough into fourths. On lightly floured surface, form each fourth into a 10x1½-inch strip; cut into 10 pieces. Roll each piece into a 9-inch rope; twist into pretzel shape. Place on prepared cookie sheet. Brush cookies with slightly beaten egg white; sprinkle with sugar. Bake at 400°F. for 5 to 7 minutes or until edges are light golden brown. 40 cookies.

HIGH ALTITUDE—Above 3500 Feet: No change.

NUTRITION INFORMATION PER SERVING

SERVING SIZE: 1 COOKIE		PERCENT U.S. RDA PER SERVING	
CALORIES	70	PROTEIN	*
PROTEIN	1g	VITAMIN A	2%
CARBOHYDRATE	8g	VITAMIN C	*
FAT	4g	THIAMINE	2%
CHOLESTEROL	30mg	RIBOFLAVIN	2%
SODIUM	40mg	NIACIN	2%
POTASSIUM	20mg	CALCIUM	*
		IRON	2%

*Contains less than 2% of the U.S. RDA of this nutrient.

Scandinavians love to use almonds in their baking. The almond flavor has made these bars a holiday favorite either at breakfast or as a dessert.

Crescent Almond Kringler Bars

8-oz. can Pillsbury Refrigerated Quick Crescent Dinner Rolls
⅔ cup water
⅓ cup margarine or butter
⅔ cup Pillsbury's BEST® All Purpose or Unbleached Flour
2 eggs
¼ cup powdered sugar
¼ teaspoon almond extract
¼ cup chopped blanched almonds
FROSTING
1 cup powdered sugar
2 tablespoons margarine or butter, softened
1 tablespoon milk
½ teaspoon almond extract
¼ cup chopped blanched or sliced almonds

Heat oven to 350°F. On ungreased cookie sheet, unroll dough into 2 long rectangles. Overlap long sides to form 12x8-inch rectangle; firmly press perforations to seal. In small saucepan, heat water and margarine to boiling. Lightly spoon flour into measuring cup; level off. Remove from heat; immediately add flour, stirring until smooth. Add eggs one at a time, beating well after each addition. Stir in powdered sugar and almond extract. Fold in almonds; spread mixture evenly over dough. Bake at 350°F. for 20 to 25 minutes or until light golden brown and puffy. Cool completely.

In small bowl, combine all frosting ingredients except almonds until smooth; spread over cooled bars. Sprinkle with almonds. Cut into bars. 24 bars.

NUTRITION INFORMATION PER SERVING

SERVING SIZE: 1 BAR		PERCENT U.S. RDA PER SERVING	
CALORIES	120	PROTEIN	2%
PROTEIN	2g	VITAMIN A	2%
CARBOHYDRATE	13g	VITAMIN C	*
FAT	7g	THIAMINE	4%
CHOLESTEROL	25mg	RIBOFLAVIN	2%
SODIUM	160mg	NIACIN	2%
POTASSIUM	40mg	CALCIUM	2%
		IRON	2%

*Contains less than 2% of the U.S. RDA of this nutrient.

Rum is a popular flavoring in German cookies. Here it is combined with a wonderful blend of spices in a crisp, slice-and-bake cookie.

German Spice Cookies

¼ cup chopped raisins
2 tablespoons dark rum
½ cup sugar
⅓ cup firmly packed brown sugar
¾ cup margarine or butter, softened
¼ cup buttermilk*
2¼ cups Pillsbury's BEST® All Purpose or Unbleached Flour
¾ teaspoon baking soda
¼ teaspoon salt
1 teaspoon cinnamon
1 teaspoon nutmeg
1 teaspoon coriander
¼ teaspoon cloves
¼ cup chopped maraschino cherries, well drained

In small bowl, combine raisins and rum; let stand 15 minutes. In large bowl, beat sugar, brown sugar and margarine until light and fluffy. Add buttermilk; blend well. Lightly spoon flour into measuring cup; level off. In medium bowl, combine flour, baking soda, salt, cinnamon, nutmeg, coriander and cloves. Stir in flour mixture; mix well. Stir in raisin mixture and cherries. On piece of waxed paper, form dough into roll 12x2-inches. Wrap in waxed paper; freeze dough 2 hours or until firm.

Heat oven to 350°F. Slice frozen dough into ¼-inch slices. Place 1 inch apart on ungreased cookie sheets. Bake at 350°F. for 10 to 15 minutes or until set. Cool 1 minute; remove from cookie sheets. 4 dozen cookies.

TIPS: *To substitute for buttermilk, use ¾ teaspoon vinegar or lemon juice plus milk to make ¼ cup.

Cookie dough may be wrapped in foil and stored in freezer up to 6 weeks.

HIGH ALTITUDE—Above 3500 Feet: Increase flour to 2½ cups. Bake as directed above.

NUTRITION INFORMATION PER SERVING

SERVING SIZE: 1 COOKIE		PERCENT U.S. RDA PER SERVING	
CALORIES	70	PROTEIN	*
PROTEIN	1g	VITAMIN A	2%
CARBOHYDRATE	9g	VITAMIN C	*
FAT	3g	THIAMINE	2%
CHOLESTEROL	0mg	RIBOFLAVIN	*
SODIUM	65mg	NIACIN	*
POTASSIUM	25mg	CALCIUM	*
		IRON	*

*Contains less than 2% of the U.S. RDA of this nutrient.

A light, delicate cookie that has worldwide appeal.

French Buttercream Cookies

1½ cups powdered sugar
1 cup butter or margarine, softened
1 teaspoon vanilla
1 egg
2¼ cups Pillsbury's BEST® All Purpose or Unbleached Flour
1 teaspoon baking soda
1 teaspoon cream of tartar
¼ teaspoon salt
Food coloring
Colored sugar

Heat oven to 350°F. Grease cookie sheets. In large bowl, beat powdered sugar, butter, vanilla and egg until well blended. Lightly spoon flour into measuring cup; level off. Stir in flour, baking soda, cream of tartar and salt; mix well. If desired, tint dough with a few drops of food coloring. Cover dough with plastic wrap. Refrigerate about 1 hour or until firm.

Shape dough into 1-inch balls. Place 2 inches apart on prepared cookie sheets. Flatten with fork; sprinkle with colored sugar. Bake at 350°F. for 5 to 8 minutes or until set but not brown. DO NOT OVERBAKE. Cool 1 minute; remove from cookie sheets. Store loosely covered. 6 dozen cookies.

HIGH ALTITUDE—Above 3500 Feet: No change.

NUTRITION INFORMATION PER SERVING

SERVING SIZE: 1 COOKIE		PERCENT U.S. RDA PER SERVING	
CALORIES	45	PROTEIN	*
PROTEIN	0g	VITAMIN A	*
CARBOHYDRATE	5g	VITAMIN C	*
FAT	3g	THIAMINE	*
CHOLESTEROL	10mg	RIBOFLAVIN	*
SODIUM	50mg	NIACIN	*
POTASSIUM	5mg	CALCIUM	*
		IRON	*

*Contains less than 2% of the U.S. RDA of this nutrient.

Here's a new flavor twist to these decorative Swedish cookies. A special tool called a rosette iron is used to fry the batter in hot oil, forming delicately shaped cookies.

Apple-Cinnamon Rosettes

1 cup Pillsbury's BEST® All
     Purpose or Unbleached Flour
1 tablespoon sugar
½ teaspoon salt
½ teaspoon cinnamon
¼ teaspoon nutmeg
1 cup apple juice
1 egg
1 tablespoon oil
  Oil for deep frying
  Powdered sugar

Lightly spoon flour into measuring cup; level off. In small bowl, combine flour, sugar, salt, cinnamon and nutmeg. Add apple juice, egg and oil. Beat with wire whisk or rotary beater until smooth.

In deep fryer or heavy saucepan, heat 3 to 4 inches of oil to 365°F. Place rosette iron in hot oil for about 30 to 60 seconds or until iron is hot. Gently dip hot iron into batter. DO NOT ALLOW BATTER TO RUN OVER TOP OF IRON. Return iron to hot oil, immersing completely for 25 to 30 seconds or until rosette is crisp and lightly browned.* Remove from oil; allow oil to drip off. Gently slip rosette off iron onto paper towels. Cool completely. Dust with powdered sugar. Store in tightly covered container. 4 dozen rosettes.

TIP: *If rosettes drop from mold, oil is too hot.
     If rosettes are soft, increase frying time.

NUTRITION INFORMATION PER SERVING

SERVING SIZE: 1 ROSETTE		PERCENT U.S. RDA PER SERVING	
CALORIES	45	PROTEIN	*
PROTEIN	0g	VITAMIN A	*
CARBOHYDRATE	3g	VITAMIN C	2%
FAT	4g	THIAMINE	*
CHOLESTEROL	6mg	RIBOFLAVIN	*
SODIUM	25mg	NIACIN	*
POTASSIUM	10mg	CALCIUM	*
		IRON	*

*Contains less than 2% of the U.S. RDA of this nutrient.

Apple-Cinnamon Rosettes

The Greek name for these cookies is
Melomakarouna. They are a tender,
spicy cookie with a honey glaze and
topping of walnuts.

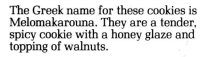

Greek Honey Spice Cookies

COOKIES
- ¼ cup sugar
- ½ cup margarine or butter, softened
- ¼ cup oil
- 1 egg yolk
- 2 tablespoons cognac or orange juice
- 1 tablespoon grated lemon peel
- 2¼ cups Pillsbury's BEST® All Purpose or Unbleached Flour
- ½ teaspoon baking soda
- ¼ teaspoon cinnamon
- ⅓ teaspoon cloves
- ¼ cup milk

HONEY SYRUP
- 1 cup sugar
- ½ cup water
- ½ cup honey
- 2 tablespoons finely chopped walnuts

In large bowl, beat sugar, margarine and
oil until light and fluffy. Add egg yolk,
cognac and lemon peel; blend well.
Lightly spoon flour into measuring cup;
level off. In medium bowl, combine flour,
baking soda, cinnamon and cloves. Add
alternately with milk to sugar mixture,
beating well after each addition. Cover
with plastic wrap; refrigerate at least
2 hours or overnight.

Heat oven to 325°F. Using level
tablespoon of dough, shape into ovals
about 1½ inches long. Place 1 inch apart
on ungreased cookie sheets. Bake at
325°F. for 20 to 25 minutes or until light
golden brown. Immediately remove from
cookie sheets; cool completely.

In small saucepan, combine sugar, water
and honey; bring to a boil. Boil gently
uncovered for 10 minutes. Lower heat to
keep warm. Using two forks, dip cookies
into the hot honey syrup, coating
completely; drain on wire rack. Sprinkle
cookies with walnuts. Store loosely
covered. 3½ dozen cookies.

🖼 FOOD PROCESSOR DIRECTIONS:
Lightly spoon flour into measuring cup;
level off. Place flour, baking soda,
cinnamon and cloves in food processor
bowl with metal blade. Cover; process
until well mixed. Remove; set aside. Cut
room-temperature margarine into 1-inch
pieces. Place in same food processor
bowl along with sugar, oil, egg yolk,
cognac and lemon peel. Cover; process
until light and fluffy. Scrape down sides
of bowl. Add milk. Cover; process with
on/off turns until blended. Scrape down
sides of bowl. Add flour mixture. Cover;
process using on/off turns just until flour
is incorporated. (Do not over process or
cookies will be tough.) Cover with plastic
wrap; refrigerate at least 2 hours or
overnight. Continue as directed above.

HIGH ALTITUDE—Above 3500 Feet:
No change.

NUTRITION INFORMATION PER SERVING

SERVING SIZE: 1 COOKIE		PERCENT U.S. RDA PER SERVING	
CALORIES	100	PROTEIN	*
PROTEIN	1g	VITAMIN A	2%
CARBOHYDRATE	15g	VITAMIN C	*
FAT	4g	THIAMINE	2%
CHOLESTEROL	6mg	RIBOFLAVIN	*
SODIUM	40mg	NIACIN	*
POTASSIUM	15mg	CALCIUM	*
		IRON	2%

*Contains less than 2% of the U.S. RDA of this nutrient.

A quick-to-make bar with an intriguing blend of flavors.

Viennese Walnut Bars

BASE
1 pkg. Pillsbury Plus Butter Recipe Cake Mix
2 tablespoons margarine or butter, softened
3-oz. pkg. cream cheese, softened
1 cup chopped walnuts
6-oz. pkg. (1 cup) semi-sweet chocolate chips

TOPPING
1½ teaspoons instant coffee granules or crystals
1 teaspoon water
¼ cup margarine or butter, softened
½ cup firmly packed brown sugar
2 eggs
½ cup chopped walnuts
Powdered sugar, if desired

Heat oven to 350°F. Grease 13x9-inch pan. In large bowl, combine 2 cups of the cake mix, 2 tablespoons margarine and cream cheese at low speed until crumbly. Press in bottom of prepared pan. Sprinkle with 1 cup walnuts and chocolate chips.

In same bowl, dissolve instant coffee in water. Add remaining cake mix, ¼ cup margarine, brown sugar and eggs; blend well. Spoon topping evenly over base; carefully spread to cover completely. Sprinkle with ½ cup walnuts.

Bake at 350°F. for 25 to 30 minutes or until light golden brown and center is set. Cool; sprinkle lightly with powdered sugar. Cut into bars. 36 bars.

HIGH ALTITUDE—Above 3500 Feet: No change.

NUTRITION INFORMATION PER SERVING

SERVING SIZE: 1 BAR		PERCENT U.S. RDA PER SERVING	
CALORIES	160	PROTEIN	2%
PROTEIN	2g	VITAMIN A	2%
CARBOHYDRATE	18g	VITAMIN C	*
FAT	9g	THIAMINE	2%
CHOLESTEROL	20mg	RIBOFLAVIN	*
SODIUM	100mg	NIACIN	*
POTASSIUM	65mg	CALCIUM	2%
		IRON	4%

*Contains less than 2% of the U.S. RDA of this nutrient.

This elegant and colorful thumbprint cookie can be varied by using your favorite preserves or jelly.

· Italian Nut Balls

¾ cup sugar
¾ cup margarine or butter, softened
½ teaspoon almond extract
½ teaspoon vanilla
2 eggs, separated
2 cups Pillsbury's BEST® All Purpose or Unbleached Flour
1 teaspoon salt
1 to 1½ cups finely chopped pistachios or other nuts
½ cup preserves or jelly

Heat oven to 350°F. Grease cookie sheets. In large bowl, beat at low speed sugar, margarine, almond extract, vanilla and egg yolks until well blended. Lightly spoon flour into measuring cup; level off. Stir in flour and salt; mix well. If necessary, refrigerate dough about 30 minutes for easier handling.

Shape dough into 1-inch balls. Dip balls into egg whites, then nuts. Place 2 inches apart on prepared cookie sheets. With thumb, make deep indentation in center of each cookie. Bake at 350°F. for 10 to 12 minutes or until firm to the touch and lightly browned. DO NOT OVERBAKE. Immediately remove from cookie sheets. While warm, fill centers with ½ teaspoon preserves. Allow preserves to set before storing cookies. 3 to 4 dozen cookies.

HIGH ALTITUDE—Above 3500 Feet: No change.

NUTRITION INFORMATION PER SERVING

SERVING SIZE: 1 COOKIE		PERCENT U.S. RDA PER SERVING	
CALORIES	90	PROTEIN	2%
PROTEIN	2g	VITAMIN A	2%
CARBOHYDRATE	10g	VITAMIN C	*
FAT	5g	THIAMINE	4%
CHOLESTEROL	10mg	RIBOFLAVIN	*
SODIUM	80mg	NIACIN	*
POTASSIUM	55mg	CALCIUM	*
		IRON	2%

*Contains less than 2% of the U.S. RDA of this nutrient.

Nutrition Information

Pillsbury's NUTRI-CODED system can help you in your daily food planning.** Below are guidelines:

SERVING SIZE: This has been determined as a typical serving for each recipe.

CALORIES: The amount of calories a person needs is determined by age, size and activity level. The recommended daily allowances generally are: 1800-2400 for women and children 4 to 10 years of age and 2400-2800 for men.

PROTEIN: The amount of protein needed daily is determined by age and size; the general U.S. RDA is 65 grams for adults and children of at least 4 years of age.

CARBOHYDRATE, FAT, CHOLESTEROL, SODIUM, AND POTASSIUM: Recommended Dietary Allowances (RDA) for these nutrients have not been determined; however, the carbohydrate should be adequate so the body does not burn protein for energy. The American Heart Association recommendation for those who wish to restrict dietary cholesterol is for a daily intake that is less than 100 milligrams per 1000 calories and not exceeding a total of 300 milligrams.

PERCENT U.S. RDA PER SERVING: For a nutritionally balanced diet, choose recipes which will provide 100% of the U.S. Recommended Daily Allowance for each nutrient.

Pillsbury Guidelines for Calculating the Nutrition Information:

When the ingredient listing gives one or more options, the first ingredient listed is the one analyzed.

When a range is given for an ingredient, the larger amount is analyzed.

When ingredients are listed as "if desired", these ingredients are included in the nutrition information.

Serving suggestions listed in the ingredients are calculated in the nutrition information.

When each bread recipe is analyzed, a serving of yeast-leavened bread is a 1-oz. slice and a quick bread serving, 1/16 of the loaf. Recipes that vary are indicated.

Symbol Meanings:

The following symbols are used in relation to the nutrition data:

*   Less than 2% of the nutrient

<1   Less than one gram (or milligram) of the nutrient

Any questions regarding nutrition information in this book should be addressed to:

The Pillsbury Company
Pillsbury Center—Suite 2866
Minneapolis, Minnesota 55402

**The primary source for values used in this program is the revised Agriculture Handbook No. 8 and is only as correct and complete as the information supplies.

NOTE FOR PEOPLE WITH SPECIAL DIETARY NEEDS: CONSULT YOUR PHYSICIAN REGARDING RELIANCE ON THE NUTRITION INFORMATION IN THIS BOOK.
Every effort has been made to ensure the accuracy of this information. However, The Pillsbury Company does not guarantee its suitability for specific medically imposed diets.

Index

D

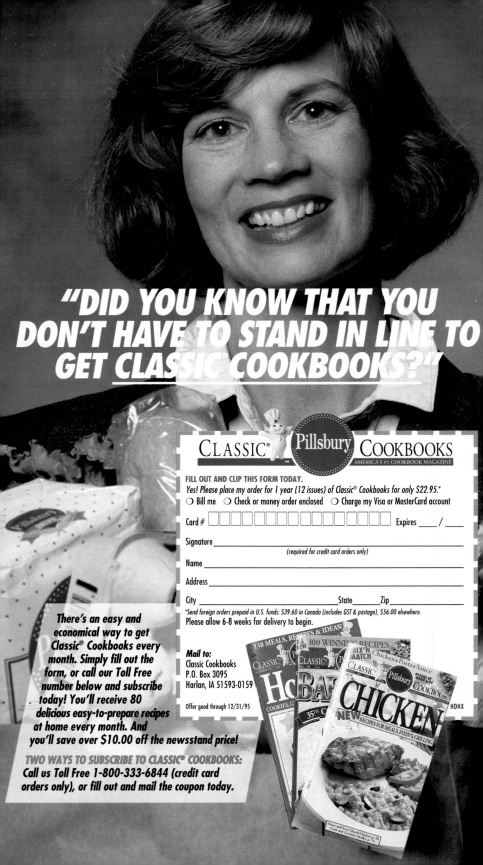